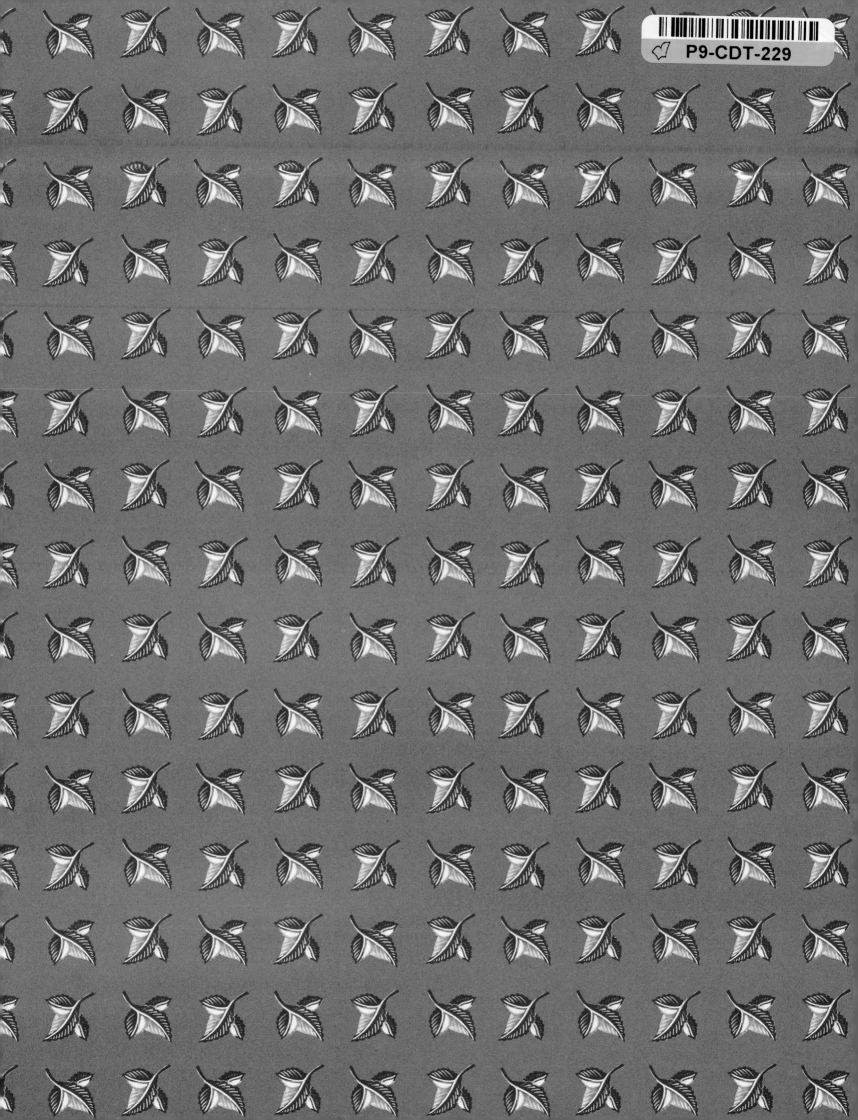

P9-CDT-229

The Best
CHRISTMAS
Ever

The Best CHRISTMAS *Ever*

FESTIVE FOOD, GIFTS AND
DECORATIONS TO GIVE AND ENJOY

PAMELA WESTLAND

SMITHMARK

This edition published in 1995 by
SMITHMARK Publishers Inc.
16 East 32nd Street
New York
NY 10016

SMITHMARK Books are available for bulk purchase
for sales promotion and for premium use.
For details write or call the Manager of Special Sales,
SMITHMARK Publishers Inc.
16 East 32nd Street, New York, NY 10016: (212) 532-6600

ISBN 0-8317-3076-5

Editorial Director: Joanna Lorenz
Project Editor: Lindsay Porter
Designer: Tony Paine
Photographer: Nelson Hargreaves

Printed in Singapore by
Star Standard Industries Pte. Ltd.

The material in this book
previously appeared in *Celebrating Christmas*

CONTENTS

INTRODUCTION

The celebration of Christmas is deeply woven into the fabric of family life, and often comprises the most precious childhood memories. Many of these memories are centred on the kitchen which, as the culinary preparations get under way in the helter-skelter run-up to Christmas, more than ever becomes the heart of the home. We may cherish memories of stirring the Christmas pudding and making a secret wish; of scraping out the mixing bowl and delighting in the warm spiciness of the blend; of rolling out left-over pastry into personal pies and, later, of making gingerbread men to hang on the tree and give to our friends.

Other memories might be of hand-made Christmas cards for friends and family, of making presents with paper and paint, needle and thread, or clay and beads; and of thinking up ingenious ways of gift wrapping.

The text and the photographs throughout this book should help to rekindle your own memories of family Christmas celebrations, and fire you with renewed enthusiasm to create new ones.

There are sections devoted to decking the home with holly and ivy, mistletoe, fruit, flowers and candles in traditional and original ways and ideas to make the most of Christmas presents.

For children a section of projects and ideas have been devised especially for them, brilliant paper-flower designs; step-by-step photographs of making gingerbread house biscuits; candy decorations to hang on the tree and adorn the table, and stunning papercraft designs for window panels and candleholders.

Eat, drink and be merry is the theme of the following section, itself a celebration of Christmas imbibing, from Champagne cocktails to spicy mulls, sparkling fruit cups to foamy egg flips. There are also recipes and ideas for appetizers and snacks to serve with drinks of all kinds to help you plan a galaxy of trouble-free gatherings.

The smooth running of the Christmas catering programme calls for a fair amount of advance planning and, nearer the day, meticulous timing. The final sections of the book take you through the tasks of making your Christmas puddings, mincemeat and cakes and all the extra cakes and cookies, candies and sweets you will need to entertain in style.

The wealth of practical projects and stunning colour photographs throughout the book will inspire you to share the kind of Christmas that memories are made of.

Pamela Westland

DECORATING FOR CHRISTMAS

The way homes are decorated for Christmas today owes everything to tradition and offers a great deal to excite the imagination.

In this section, there are ideas for decorations composed largely of materials gathered from the garden and the countryside, of vibrant hips and berries, gleaming fruit and nuts and papery dried flowers and bracts. Some of the decorations are embellished with silver and golden paints and shimmering ribbons, and there are ideas for dressing the Christmas tree in the Victorian manner, with fruits and flowers and gingerbread and twinkling lights — in ways which will fire your own enthusiasm.

WELCOME WREATHS

THE TRADITION of hanging evergreens and decorative wreaths on the door, and of suspending 'kissing rings' in a hall or living room, has its origins in pagan times. Ancient peoples believed that evergreens had magical powers because they retained their leaves in winter when other branches were bare. They came to symbolize eternal life, as did wreaths, rings and circles garlanded with plants. Holly, ivy and mistletoe were also seen as powerful life symbols because they bore fruit in the winter. They were hung in people's homes and exchanged as gifts in the hope of warding off evil spirits and bringing eternal good fortune.

The decorative use of these plants outlived the ancient beliefs in their supposed powers, and they were adopted by the early Christians, too; though not without some misgivings. The early Fathers of the Christian Church were fearful that 'bringing in the holly' at Christmastime would keep alive memories of pagan rituals, and for several centuries the use of 'green boughs' as a winter decoration was banned by the Church. A similar attitude was adopted by the Puritan Fathers in New England, who took a firm line on the association between Christmas and evergreens until as late as the early nineteenth century.

All that is history, and for many families throughout the world, both Christians and non-Christians, the festival would not be complete without a holly wreath hung on the door as a sign of welcome and good fortune, and a sprig of mistletoe in the hall. From its ancient beginnings as a fertility charm, a supposed cure-all for countless illnesses and a force against evil, mistletoe now has purely romantic associations. At the beginning of this century every young man who

stole a kiss under the mistletoe bough or kissing ring had to pluck a berry from its depths. When there were no more berries left, the kissing had to stop.

Over the centuries, evergreens came to be decorated with ribbon bows and other embellishments and in Victorian times red and green tartan ribbons, which matched the vibrant colours of the holly itself, became fashionable. In those days too it was the custom to add candies and bon-bons, tiny toys for the children and other purely decorative and fanciful items to the basic evergreen wreaths. This delightful practice continues today.

COUNTRY WREATHS

Today, creative expression is given free rein, and Christmas decorations, whilst still deeply rooted in tradition, make imaginative use of all types of plant material.

Preserving the fruits of the countryside or the garden in readiness for Christmas is one of the most pleasant of preparatory tasks. Rosehips – if they survive the onslaught of winter-hungry birds – can be preserved in a solution of glycerin and water to rival the brilliance of holly berries. Preserved rosehips and other fruits and seeds such as rowan (mountain ash), hawthorn and pyracantha (firethorn) berries can be incorporated into an evergreen wreath to supplement or replace holly berries, or used alone in all their glory. Rosehips inserted into a twisted willow wreath form make a bold statement that, where Christmas decorations are concerned, bright is beautiful. This is also true of cranberries, a vibrant, and popular component of Christmas decorations.

RIGHT: Since time immemorial people have hung wreaths composed of holly, ivy and other evergreens as a symbol of good fortune, and of welcome. The addition of tartan ribbon was especially popular in Victorian times.

OPPOSITE: Vibrant rosehips rival holly berries as the brightest plant materials around. Cut short the stems and push them between the intertwined stems of a willow (as here) or vine wreath form. A few stray rose leaves add a natural look.

COUNTRY WREATH

In the time-honoured tradition of natural wreaths, this design blends the contrasting colours and textures of horse chestnut and sweet chestnut cases, dried red chillies and bunches of cinnamon quills.

EQUIPMENT
* raffia
* fine silver wire
* medium stub wires
* wire cutters
* scissors
* 25cm/10in vine wreath form
* hot glue gun

DECORATIVE MATERIALS
* cinnamon sticks
* dried red chillies
* horse chestnuts
* sweet chestnut cases
* 7.5cm/3in-wide shiny ribbon

1 Tie short cinnamon sticks into bundles with raffia and thread small chillies in clusters onto fine silver wire.

2 Cut the stub wires in half, bend into U-shapes to make staples and push through the raffia ties. Fix the cinnamon bunches to the wreath form by pushing the wires between the vine twigs. Glue the horse chestnuts and sweet chestnut cases at random around the ring, adding the long red chillies last, as colour accents.

3 Tie the ribbon in a bow, and attach to the wreath with a stub wire (floral pin). Because it is composed of weatherproof materials, the wreath could be hung on an exterior wall.

ALL AGLOW

The contrasting characteristics of matt and spiky juniper bunches and golden, glowing quinces combine to compose a striking wall decoration.

1 Cut the evergreen stems to about 20cm/8in long and gather them into bunches of three, four or five, depending on thickness. Tie the twine to the ring frame and bind on the bunches so that the tips of one cover the stems of the next. Continue until the frame is covered.

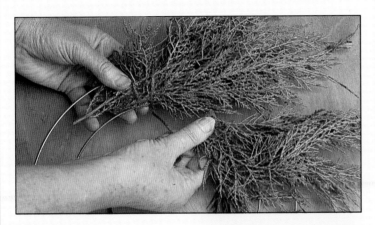

2 Measure the heavy-gauge wire around the inside of the completed evergreen ring and, allowing for a short overlap, cut it to size. Thread the quinces onto the wire and, when it is complete, push the two ends into the first and last of the fruits to be threaded. If the wire will not hold its position, wire the two fruits together at the back with a stub wire.

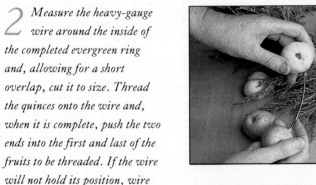

3 Bind the evergreen and the fruit rings together with silver wire, making a loop for hanging. The decoration may be hung on a door, or a wall, either inside or outside. It is especially effective in a kitchen or living room, where the aroma of the fruit may be appreciated.

EQUIPMENT

* florists' scissors
* binding twine
* 25cm/10in wire ring frame (from florists)
* heavy-gauge flexible wire
* wire cutters
* medium stub wires
* fine silver wire

DECORATIVE MATERIALS

* evergreens such as juniper (cypress or yew would give a similar effect)
* small quinces

GLISTENING WREATHS

Just as holly and ivy leaves were once valued for their sheen and the consequential brilliance they brought to the house in the dark days of winter, so artificial glitter sprays, paints and powders have come to play a significant role in Christmas decorations. Although all that glisters may not indeed be gold, a spatter of gold or silver paint here and there, as a highlight on evergreen or fallen leaves, on nuts, dried seedheads and flowers (and even on gift wrapping paper) transforms and uplifts decorations of all kinds.

It is a matter of personal preference whether this decorative Midas touch is employed to give the merest hint of gold – as if, for example, a bunch of holly had been spattered by golden raindrops – or is used for a complete cover-up for a look of gilded luxury. Both approaches lay claim to decorative merit.

The wreath of mixed evergreens, wheat and linseed (flaxseed) combines the best of both worlds in decorative terms. The bunches of seedheads are totally gilded, the ivy, eucalyptus and false flowers only splattered with gold, and the cypress left in its natural state.

A similar all-and-nothing combination of gilded and not gilded materials has been used on the nut ring, where gold-sprayed walnuts and almonds contrast vividly with the natural colours and textures of unsprayed pecans, hazelnuts (filberts) and nutmegs formed into clusters and wired into the natural willow ring.

Ribbon bows and trails can do much to add a sparkle or a colour highlight to evergreen and other decorative wreaths. Choose them as carefully as you would fashion accessories. Your choice of ribbons determines whether a wreath has an informal and countrified look (check gingham typifies this style); has a more elegant and classic feel, which the use of tartan ribbon does so much to promote; or has the frankly festive air of the Christmas party season. Sparkly gold and silver woven thread ribbons, ribbons with a shot-silk effect, and printed metallic ribbons are all delightfully luxurious and festive options.

LEFT: A natural willow ring, gold spray-paint, a hot glue gun and a handful of nuts are all you need to create this striking table design. Add a glittering bow as an eye-catching finishing touch. You can glue it to the ring frame or fix it in position with a bent stub wire.

MISTLETOE RING

A symbol of romance and Christmas frivolities, mistletoe is combined with other evergreens and gilded seedheads in a wayward wreath that is at once elegant and casual.

EQUIPMENT
* binding twine
* gold spray-paint
* 30cm/12in stem wreath form
* medium stub wires
* wire cutters
* scissors

DECORATIVE MATERIALS
* wheat stalks
* linseed (flaxseed)
* evergreens such as cypress, ivy, mistletoe and eucalyptus
* artificial Christmas roses
* 7.5cm/3in-wide shiny ribbon

1 Gather the wheat stalks into bunches of three or four and bind the stems. Form the linseed (flaxseed) into bunches of uneven lengths, to give the design its wispy outline, and bind the stems. Lightly spray the wheat, linseed (flaxseed), artificial Christmas roses and a few of the evergreens with gold paint.

2 Using mixed bunches of the plant materials, secure them to the ring with half a stub wire bent to make a U-shaped staple. Continue all around the ring, so that the heads of each bunch cover the stems and staples of the one before.

3 Push the stems of the Christmas roses into the ring at irregular intervals. Shape 2 ribbon bows, trim the ends by cutting them slantwise and fix them to the wreath with stub wire staples.

CANDLE WREATHS

The combination of candles and evergreens in a wreath formation is most powerfully expressed in the symbolic Advent wreath. By tradition in the Christian church – and it is a tradition that is carried out both in churches and at home – one of the four candles is lighted on each of the four Sundays prior to Christmas. Not only does this practice have a deep religious significance, but it results in an asymmetrical design brought about by the unevenness of the candles.

The interpretation of an Advent candle wreath illustrated on these pages breaks with the visual though not the religious tradition, and uses a partnership of delicate flowers and pastel candles. The blend of fresh flowers is a herald of spring, and the slender tapers are in a myriad of colours from traditional holly green and berry red to palest apricot and pink. A design like this would make an eye-catching table centre-piece, a stunning focal point on a sideboard or side table or an inspiring, outward-looking decoration on a wide windowsill.

LEFT: Adopt the Victorian tradition and embellish an Advent ring with tiny gift parcels to be opened on Christmas Eve. The decoration is made on a pre-formed absorbent foam ring covered first with small sprays of evergreen – it could be variegated holly, ivy or box (boxwood) – and the snippings of sea lavender dyed pink, pink rosebuds and dried everlasting flowers. One candle is lit on each of the Sundays during Advent.

A Ring for all Seasons

A fresh flower decoration with four pale-coloured tapers is inspired by the tradition of an Advent ring. This one combines winter-flowering laurustinus (viburnum) and summery blooms with sprays of minute white flowers, like pretty snowflakes.

EQUIPMENT

* 25cm/10in diameter absorbent foam ring, soaked in water
* 25cm/10in in diameter
* florists' scissors

DECORATIVE MATERIALS

* selection of flowers such as spray carnations, Peruvian lilies, freesias, gypsophila (baby's breath)
* flowering shrub such as laurustinus (viburnum)
* 4 slender tapers

3 Fill in the ring until it has a pleasing balance of colour, and add short sprays of gypsophila (baby's breath) all around, like delicate snowflakes. Insert the tapers firmly into the foam at the chosen focal point.

1 Cut short sprays of the flowering shrub and arrange them around the foam so that they largely cover the inside and outside rims. Position the Peruvian lilies around the ring so that they are evenly spaced.

2 Arrange a special feature at one end of the ring, where it will surround the tapers and become the focal point. In this design, deep pink freesias were used for this purpose.

ALTERNATIVE CHRISTMAS TREES

EVER SINCE people began bringing boughs of evergreens into their homes an unrecorded number of years ago, the tree has held a place of honour – first at the winter solstice festival and then at Christmas. Boughs of greenery were hung over doors to represent both welcome and hoped-for good fortune. On walls they were sometimes arranged to resemble the shape of the living tree.

However, the custom of transplanting an entire evergreen tree and installing it as the focal point of the Christmas festivities is a comparatively recent innovation. Prince Albert, Queen Victoria's husband, introduced the idea to Britain in 1841, and brought with it a number of other Christmas customs from his native Germany.

If you decide this year to have a natural tree, you may still have room for another one – a designer tree that clings to the spirit of Christmas past and yet explores the creative possibilities of the concept. The projects illustrated are certain to tempt the most confirmed traditionalist!

LEFT: This tree is composed on a pre-formed foam ball shape and the clumps of lichen are fixed with stub-wire staples (floral pins). The harvest includes gilded peanuts, clusters of cinnamon sticks tied with raffia and kumquats pushed onto toothpicks.

BRIGHT AS A BERRY

Evoke the artistry of clipped hedges and shaped trees with a spherical tree design of glossy evergreens and shiny fruits.

DECORATIVE MATERIALS

* clippings of glossy evergreen such as box
* rosehips
* false berries (optional)

EQUIPMENT

* damp sphagnum moss
* 2.5cm/1in wire mesh netting
* wire cutters
* 18cm/7in-diameter flowerpot
* florists' adhesive tape
* scissors
* florists' scissors

1 *Place the moss on the wire mesh netting, turn the corners into the centre to enclose the moss and crush the wire into a ball shape. Tuck in or cut off any stray ends with wire cutters. Place the wire ball on the flower-pot and secure it with two or three short lengths of adhesive tape. Cut the evergreens to more or less equal lengths and push the stems into the wire ball.*

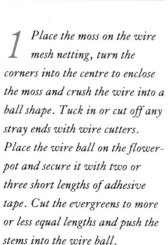

2 *Continue filling in the ball with evergreens, then push in the rosehips and, if you use them, the stems of false berries.*

3 *The evergreen 'tree' is a welcoming sight in a porch, and looks good in a fireplace or a room corner where there is enough light to enhance the colour of the leaves.*

GOLDEN HIGHLIGHTS

From yellowy-green cypress to grey-green Jerusalem sage foliage, with shiny box for highlights, this conical tree makes the most of clippings from a winter garden.

1 Place the moss on the wire mesh netting and shape it into a cone. Trim off excess netting at the top of the cone. Tuck in any stray ends of wire. Press a large piece of adhesive clay onto the base of the pinholder and press the pinholder onto the base of the basket. Push the twig onto the pinholder. Secure it by taking two wires from side to side of the basket, wrapping the wires around the twig. Place the cone on the twig and secure it by taking wires from side to side and around the twig. These will also hold the moss in place.

EQUIPMENT
* damp sphagnum moss
* 2.5cm/1in wire mesh netting
* wire cutters
* florists' adhesive clay
* pinholder
* 18cm/7in diameter cylindrical basket
* stout twig
* medium stub wires (floral pins)
* florists' scissors
* scissors

DECORATIVE MATERIALS
* selection of evergreens such as cypress, Jerusalem sage and box (boxwood)
* dried hydrangeas
* gold baubles
* 7.5cm/3in-wide ribbon

2 Arrange the evergreens to form a conical shape, and decorate the tree with clippings of dried hydrangeas and gold baubles. A glittery gold bow at the front of the basket is designed to steal the limelight.

WINDOW LIGHTS

Candles lighted in a window serve a double purpose, giving pleasure to those inside the room and others who pass by outside.

1 *Plastic foam-holders, which you can buy from florists' shops or through flower clubs, are ideal for a design of this kind. If you do not have them, wrap the soaked foam tightly in foil. To position the holders, cut strips of adhesive clay and press them to the undersides. If you are using foil-wrapped blocks, press the clay to the foil. Press the holders in place and insert blocks of soaked foam, or position the wrapped blocks. Press the candles into the foam.*

2 *Cut the stub wires in half, and bend them to make U-shaped staples to fix clumps of lichen to the foam. This will help to conceal the fixings, and give the design a wintry look. Position the planted tree if you use one.*

3 *Arrange the mixed evergreens in a dense mass of varying greens to create a 'forest floor' look. Add more greenery until all the holding materials are covered.*

EQUIPMENT

* plastic foam-holders or foil
* absorbent stem-holding foam, soaked in water
* florists' adhesive clay
* medium stub wires (floral pins)
* wire cutters

DECORATIVE MATERIALS

* green and white candles
* lichen (available from florists' shops)
* selection of mixed evergreens
* pine-cones
* fallen leaves, sprayed gold
* miniature evergreen tree, in pot (optional)

4 *Twist stub wires around a few cones and push the wires at intervals throughout the design. Lastly, arrange the gilded leaves to catch every glint of candlelight.*

CANDLE TIME

CHRISTMAS IS the time to gather your most attractive candlesticks, get in a supply of candles to tone with your seasonal colour theme, and turn the lights down low. It is also a time for improvisation, whether it is to supplement the number of candlesticks you have, or to set the scene for a special party.

You may like to incorporate candles into a large, deep swag filling a wide windowsill or mantelpiece, using thick, stubby candles raised on flowerpots concealed among the greenery. Or position tall candles to taper elegantly from a forest of twigs and pine-cones. (This decorating theme is developed in one of the preceding projects, in which both white and holly-green candles are used to seasonal effect.)

Flowerpots make practical if somewhat rustic holders for candles of all kinds – from the highly-textured beeswax ones to those in traditional colours. Select the most earthy and weatherbeaten flowerpots you have, though for the sake of the table surface they should be scrupulously clean. Plant the

candles in heavy holding material such as gravel chippings concealed under (for safety reasons) damp moss or hay. A garland of ivy trailing around the top of the flowerpot, held in place with unobtrusive blobs of clay, will add to the pastoral look while a large green and white gingham bow will add a touch more elegance.

A variety of household items can do festive duty in this way. Pottery mugs and tumblers, casseroles and baking dishes can hold a candle galaxy. A group of beakers supporting beeswax candles and surrounded by pomanders, pine-cones, polished fruits, pearly seashells or glitzy baubles would make a brilliant centre piece for the dining table or a focal point on a side table.

Plain white altar candles, beautiful in their simplicity, can be trimmed with evergreens, berries and bows to stand as a sign of welcome in a window or, again, as a table centre-piece. Snippings from larger decorations co-ordinate with the candles and at no extra expense.

VERY NEARLY VERDIGRIS

Transform bargain-shop candlesticks with this verdigris look-alike technique. Real verdigris is the green deposit that forms on copper or brass that has been exposed to the elements and oxidized. This interpretation will weather any storm!

EQUIPMENT
* candlestick
* small paintbrushes
* acrylic paints in green, gold and bronze
* turpentine (optional)
* varnish (optional)

1 Paint the candlestick with a base coat of bronze, using criss-crossing brush strokes for an uneven, textured finish. Allow paint to dry.

TARTAN TRIM

Plain white candles enter into the Christmas spirit with a festive trim of ribbon bows and evergreens.

1 Cut short lengths of the evergreens and seedheads and bind them into mixed bunches. Place a few stems against one of the candles and bind them on with silver wire. Add more bunches, binding them on all around the candle and secure the wire. Hook on false berries, if desired. Tie around the stems with ribbon to conceal the wire. Trim the other candles in a similar way.

EQUIPMENT
* 30cm/12 in-long plain white candles
* florists' scissors
* fine silver wire

DECORATIVE MATERIALS
* snippings of evergreen
* linseed (flaxseed), sprayed gold
* artificial holly berries (optional)
* 4cm/1½in-wide and 2.5cm/ 1in-wide ribbons

2 Daub the bronze-coloured surface with green paint. If you prefer a more transparent finish, thin the paint with turpentine. Allow to dry for about 10 minutes, then daub on gold paint, again applying in uneven patches.

ABOVE: A selection of brass, enamel and earthenware candlesticks, beeswax candles and slender tapers provide informal, country-style decoration.

2 Place the candles in appropriate holders and arrange them in the centre of the dining table or on a windowsill among cuttings of mixed evergreens.

3 A verdigris-style candlestick makes an elegant flower stand when it is fitted with a small foam-holder and a piece of soaked stem-holding foam. Fix the holder to the top of the candlestick with florists' adhesive tape and arrange flowers and foliage. For a festive look, fit the candlestick with a rolled beeswax candle, a ring of glossy evergreens and a handful of cream and gold flowers.

GARLANDS AND SWAGS

FROM A luxuriant garland of blue pine and glimmering ribbon to a ring of ivy leaves wound around a hat brim; from a garland of gold-sprayed hydrangea heads to an unruly composition of twigs and baubles over a fireplace; from a neat and orderly swag of nuts, resembling an intricate wood-carving to a casual and colourful pairing of orange Chinese lanterns (winter cherry) and shimmering honesty — swags and garlands enhance our homes at Christmas in myriad ways.

Gathering the materials for the decorations can be very much a family affair – involving forays into the countryside or the garden weeks in advance of the festival to cut the evergreens and twigs and hunt for fallen cones, beech nuts, chestnut cases and all the other natural materials.

MIXED BLESSINGS

An evergreen garland bringing together a host of natural materials comes close to the beauty of the forest or wayside in winter. All you need is a touch of frost for total realism.

EQUIPMENT
* wire mesh netting (see below)
* wire cutters
* absorbent stem-holding foam, soaked in water
* knife
* florists' scissors
* secateurs (pruning shears)
* stub wires (floral pins)

DECORATIVE MATERIALS
* selection of evergreens such as pine, holly, ivy, cypress, juniper and spruce
* bare twigs such as apple and teasels
* dried ferns, sprayed gold (optional)
* large cones
* ribbon or baubles, for the centre (optional)

LEFT: Trails of ivy outlining the dresser; an arrangement of evergreens and golden lilies; and candles trimmed with ribbons and dried flowers.

1 Measure the length of the fireplace, doorway or arch to be decorated with the garland, allowing for any curve or drape you wish it to have. Cut the appropriate length of wire mesh netting, and trim it to a width of about 25cm/10in. Cut blocks of absorbent foam into 6 and place them end to end along the centre of the netting. Fold the netting over from both sides to enclose the foam and secure it by bending and twisting together the cut edges of the wires. Measure and mark the centre of the garland length.

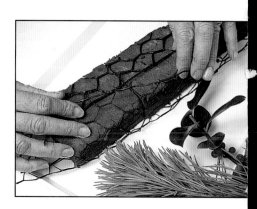

2 *Decorate the garland with the evergreens and natural materials, pushing the stems under the wire mesh and into the foam. This design is planned to have an unruly and somewhat shaggy appearance, but you could make it neater and more orderly. Continue adding more materials until you reach the end of the wire cone and the fixings are concealed. Return to the centre of the garland and decorate it outwards in the opposite direction. There is no need to match the two sides stem for stem, but the garland should have a pleasing balance.*

3 *Twist stub wires (floral pins) around a few cones and push the wires into the foam at intervals along the garland.*

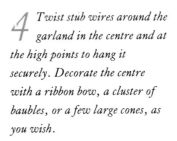

4 *Twist stub wires around the garland in the centre and at the high points to hang it securely. Decorate the centre with a ribbon bow, a cluster of baubles, or a few large cones, as you wish.*

EVERGREEN GARLAND

A garland of evergreens is the perfect seasonal decoration to transform the corner of a room, highlight a special piece of furniture or enhance a fire-place, doorway or arch.

EQUIPMENT

* thick cord or rope
* scissors
* green binding twine
* dry hay or sphagnum moss
* secateurs (pruning shears)
* hot glue gun
* stub wire (floral pins)

DECORATIVE MATERIALS

* wheat stalks, sprayed gold
* blue pine (spruce) or similar foliage
* selection of pine- and fir-cones
* 7.5cm/3in-wide glittery ribbon

1 Measure the length required for the garland, allowing for generous drapes. Cut the rope to length, tie the twine to one end and bind on handfuls of hay all along. Fasten the twine at the other end. Mark the centre of the garland.

3 Bind the bunches of wheat - at intervals along the garland. Work in this way until you reach the centre, then start at the other end, binding on one stem of the blue pine with the tip covering the end of the rope. Continue binding on more evergreens and wheat until you reach the centre of the rope.

4 Using the hot glue gun, stick the cones at intervals along the garland. You can use them to conceal or fill in any gaps in the decoration.

2 Cut the evergreen into short lengths and sprays, and bind the first one, tip facing outwards, onto the hay-covered rope. Bind on others so that the tip of each spray covers the stem end of the previous one.

5 Tie the ribbon into a bow.
Fix to the garland with a
stub wire (floral pin).

TWISTED CORD

A vertical swag of mixed
nuts, a bunch of seedheads
and two curtain tie-backs
comprise a decoration that is
reminiscent of eighteenth-
century bell-pulls.

EQUIPMENT

* 60cm/24in-long willow or
  raffia plait (braid) from
  florists
* hot glue gun or clear, quick-
  setting glue
* stub wires (floral pins)
* wire cutters
* florists' scissors

DECORATIVE MATERIALS

* selection of nuts
* dried seedheads and cones

1 Glue the nuts to the plait,
mixing the colours, shapes
and textures for a varied look.
Cones and any seedheads
which do not have
stems will have
to be wired.

2 To wire a cone,
wrap a stub wire around
the lowest 'petals', bring the two
ends of the wire together
beneath the cone and
twist them tightly.

3 To wire a lotus
seedhead, push a
stub wire through the
seedhead close to the base,
bring the two ends of
the wire together at
the base and twist.

4 Form the
seedheads
and cones into a
bunch with the heads
at varying levels and
wire them to the top of the plait
(braid). Loop two ends of the cord
tie-backs together to make one
continuous cord. Wrap it around
the top of the plait where it will
conceal the wire fixings, and twist
it around the plait. Secure the
cord with half stub wires pressed
into the back of the plait.

DRESSING THE CHRISTMAS TREE

TRIMMING THE Christmas tree is one of the most enchanting of all Christmas preparations. Weeks before the festivities begin, various members of the family can set to work making new decorations, each one maximizing his or her culinary or artistic skills. Some decorations will be so pretty that they will be brought out year after year; others so tasty that it will be touch and go whether they will survive the twelve days of Christmas.

Many families have adopted the charming custom of giving a take-home gift from the tree to anyone who calls at their home during the holiday – to visiting carol singers; friends and neighbours who drop by to deliver a Christmas card, gift or invitation; houseguests and those invited to a party. In Northern Europe, and in Holland, Germany

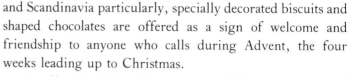

and Scandinavia particularly, specially decorated biscuits and shaped chocolates are offered as a sign of welcome and friendship to anyone who calls during Advent, the four weeks leading up to Christmas.

A tall order? Not if you start building up a stock of home-made and specially wrapped candies, gingerbread and other spiced biscuits and cookies, kumquat or tangerine pomanders and tiny inexpensive baskets filled with bought candies, dried flowers and trinkets for the children.

The decorations on these pages, and others throughout this book, will provide you with ideas for decorations to keep for the tree, and others that would make ideal gifts. Some are just asking to be eaten (when they should be suitably wrapped) and others, such as the walnut clusters and the dried mushrooms sprayed with gold paint, have moved out of the food category and into the realms of fantasy.

RIGHT: Collect pine- and fir-cones on woodland walks or buy them by the bagful in florists' shops. Wrap a wire around the top layer of 'petals', bring the wire up at the back and twist it into a loop. Finish with a gingham bow.

RIGHT: Use clear, quick-setting glue or a hot glue gun to stick nuts together in clusters. You can spray all or some of them with gold or silver paint, keep them in clusters of a single kind, or mix walnuts, pecans, hazel nuts and others. Pecans, especially, look best if some are left unsprayed; the rich pinky-red is too attractive to hide. When the glue has set, push a stub wire (floral pin) through a gap between the nuts, twist it to make a loop and tie on a decorative ribbon bow.

LEFT: Collect miniature baskets from charity shops and fill them with the most colourful candies around. A perky bow in a contrasting colour increases the eye appeal. And so do the candy sticks, hooked over the branches!

LEFT: Wedge a small piece of dry stem-holding foam into the bases of small baskets – off-cuts saved from large arrangements are suitable – and fill them to over-flowing with dried flowers and seedheads. Those shown here are Chinese lanterns (winter cherry), honesty and hops. Strawflowers, gypsophila (baby's breath) and statice would also be suitable.

ABOVE: A posy from small everlasting flowers is attached to the tree with golden ribbon.

RIGHT: Entering the realms of fantasy, dried and gold-sprayed mushrooms and toadstools make unusual tree decorations in weird and wonderful shapes. Dry the fungi in an airing cupboard or an oven at the lowest setting with the door slightly open. After spraying, tie them singly, in pairs or in groups with bright and shiny ribbons.

LEFT: Bundles of dried flowers and seedheads tied with red ribbons and strings of threaded cranberries hanging like jewelled necklaces – what could be prettier! Thread cranberries with a darning needle and double-thickness sewing thread.

RIGHT: Select gourds in all shapes and sizes and spatter-spray them with gold or silver paint. Fix a hook to the stalk and tie on a bow that will catch every flicker of light from the Christmas tree candles.

RIGHT: *White wooden curtain rings take on a new role as dried flower holders. Cut 4 slits in a Chinese lantern (winter cherry) or Cape gooseberry (physalis) case and open it out like a flower. Stick it to the base of a ring and stick a pink everlasting flower inside it, with another at the top. Tie a ribbon bow through the small metal ring.*

BELOW: *Make decorative 'candleholders' by sticking a small white cake candle, the wick burnt for a look of realism, to the base of a white curtain ring. Cut a piece of gold sequin trim to fit and stick it on the back of the ring. Add a gold-sprayed star anise seedpod at the front for a decoration certain to become a family heirloom.*

ABOVE: *Thick, shiny orange rings look good enough to eat, even when they have been dried. Cut 6mm/¼in slices from a large orange, place on a rack and dry in an oven at the lowest temperature for about 1 hour. Push a knife through just below the peel and thread with a ribbon.*

LEFT: *Tie decorative bundles of cinnamon sticks together with ribbon for a sweetly scented tree trim. Fix cranberries to the ribbon with a strong, clear adhesive, to complement the jewel-bright garlands of cranberries threaded onto sewing cotton.*

RIGHT: Pretzel sticks are tied into bundles with festive ribbon, and decorated with a gold-dusted leaf.

ABOVE: Deck the tree with the prettiest of citrus fruits, tiny egg-shaped kumquats, by threading them onto medium stub wires. Loop the circlets over the tree branches, or tie them with toning or contrasting ribbons.

LEFT AND BELOW: These traditional tree decorations are as popular and tasty as ever. Use a gingerbread cutter to cut out the basic shapes and create a variety of characters – some bald, bearded, young or old – with the icing.

BELOW: Save a few salty pretzels from the snack tray and shape them into bright tree ornaments. Or, stick circular biscuits together with fondant icing to make a hoop.

CHRISTMAS POSIES

NATURAL POSIES probably come closest of all Christmas decorations to the original concept of bringing in bunches of evergreens in celebration of the winter festival. For at their simplest such posies need be no more than a handful of leafy twigs, brilliant berries or papery bracts hanging in a doorway, over a stairwell or in a room corner.

Selecting materials for Christmas posies is influenced not only by tradition but by design considerations. A bunch of deep green ivy and holly endowed with a few berries may be strong on tradition but could appear as a dense, featureless mass if it were not spot-lit with particular sensitivity. The inclusion of a variegated component makes all the difference, and it provides the ray of lightness necessary to bring the bunch into focus. There are a great many examples of variegated holly whose leaves are tinged with cream, white or yellow; some also have well-defined yellow streaks and others – *Ilex aquilfolium bacciflava* is an example – bear sunshine-yellow berries.

Ivy, too, is a plant of many colours and, for the sake of appearances, it is worth seeking out varieties which have especially glossy leaves, are in the green-going-on-yellow colour range, or have intricate and interesting reddish-brown veining.

In a year when holly is richly endowed with berries it is a good decorative idea to strip some stalks of the leaves. This will go some way towards diminishing the all-over greenness of a bunch, maximize the vibrant impact of the berries, and yet stay within the bounds of tradition.

Breaking away from the bounds, Christmas posies can comprise a decorative wealth of other natural materials, as examples on these pages show. Gather a handful of wayward spindle twigs (cotoneaster) thick with their distinctive pinky-crimson fruits opening to show orange-scarlet seeds. With a few contrasting, yellowing leaves clinging to the branches, the posy needs no further adornment. Because of its spindly nature, it is advisable to hang such a bunch where it will be viewed against a plain wall, door or panel. Any degree of pattern on the background would impose unfair visual competition.

LEFT: As simple as can be – a bunch of spindle branches (cotoneaster) vibrant with berries.

A TOUCH OF ROMANCE

A heart-shaped frame covered with evergreen and fragrant rosemary is decorated with a posy of romantic red rosebuds and seasonal holly and ivy.

EQUIPMENT

* strong, flexible wire
* fine silver wire
* hollow wheat straw

DECORATIVE MATERIALS

* rosemary
* dried red and cream rosebuds
* honesty, holly and ivy
* 2.5cm/1in-wide ribbon

1 *Bend the wire into a circle, bind the 2 ends securely with silver wire and shape the wire frame to form a heart. Cover the frame with short sprays of rosemary, so that the tips of each bunch cover the stem ends of the one before.*

2 *Bind the dried flowers and seedheads, holly and ivy on the wheat stalk to give the appearance of a posy.*

3 *Use the wire to bind the evergreen and dried flower posy to the heart-shaped frame. Decorate the design with a flourish of shining ribbons.*

DOOR POSY

Gilded wheat and evergreens, as glittering as the ribbon bow, are formed into a welcoming door posy.

EQUIPMENT

* newspaper or scrap paper
* fine silver wire
* gold spray-paint
* scissors

DECORATIVE MATERIALS

* wheat stalks
* selection of evergreens such as blue pine (spruce), cypress, ivy and yew
* dried grasses
* 4cm/2½in-wide gold ribbon

1 Cover the work surface with newspaper or scrap paper. Gather 10 or 12 wheat stalks to form a bunch and bind them with silver wire. Spray the wheat and ivy with gold paint and leave to dry.

2 Place the largest component on the work surface and arrange the other materials over it. Bind the stems firmly together with wire and tie the ribbon to form a bow. Cut the ends slantwise.

ABOVE: Twisting hop vines with papery bracts compose a delightful posy with understated colour. A single stem of pale orange Chinese lanterns (winter cherry) and a single woody seedhead complete the design. The stems are bound with fine silver wire, concealed beneath the ribbon.

SALT DOUGH DECORATIONS

Attractive but inedible salt dough decorations, thought to have originated in Germany, are popular throughout Northern Europe where they are frequently exchanged as Christmas gifts. Following this basic recipe you can make a posy as shown in the photograph; simple plaited rings as candleholders or tree decorations; or a bell, Christmas tree or other festive shapes cut out with cookie cutters.

INGREDIENTS
*200g/7oz/2 cups plain
(all-purpose) flour
200g/7oz/2 cups salt
1 tsp glycerin
100ml/4fl oz/½ cup cold water*

1 Pre-heat the oven to 100°C/200°F/Gas ¼. Sift the flour and salt into a mixing bowl, add the glycerin and slowly pour on the water, mixing continuously to form a firm but pliable dough. Do not make the dough too wet, or it will be too sticky to handle. Dust a pastry board with flour and roll out the dough to a thickness of about 6mm/¼in.

EQUIPMENT
* sieve (flour sifter)
* mixing bowl
* pastry board
* rolling pin
* non-stick baking paper
* knife
* pastry brush
* metal skewer
* spatula
* baking sheet
* cooling rack
* paintbrush
* clear polyurethane varnish
* 2.5cm/1in-wide ribbon

5 Transfer the baked decoration onto a wire rack to cool. Brush the posy all over, on the front and back surfaces, with varnish. Leave to dry for 24 hours, then apply another coat. Leave to dry again, then insert the ribbon and tie a bow at the top.

2 Cut the basic shape of the posy, almost that of an hour glass. Cover the shape with non-stick baking paper while you shape the rest of the design. Cut out the leaves and mark the veins with the point of a knife. Cut thin strips of dough and roll them around to form rose shapes. Cut out and shape the flat-faced flowers and the berries. Roll some dough into thin sausage shapes for the stalks. Cut a rectangle for the bow and pinch it into shape between your thumb and forefinger.

3 Brush the background shape with water and arrange the decorations. Use a skewer to push a hole at the top of the design.

4 Lift the posy onto a well-floured baking sheet and bake in the pre-heated oven at 100°C/ 200°F/Gas ¼ for 30 minutes. Increase the temperature to 150°C/300°F/Gas 2 and continue baking for about 2 hours, or until the decoration is dry and hard all the way through.

CHRISTMAS GIFTS TO MAKE

What do a scented candle, a zingy flower arrangement in a cone-covered basket, a rosebud pomander, a box of Turkish delight and a jar of pickled vegetables have in common? They are just a few of the many suggestions for gifts you can make throughout the year to delight your family and friends, and to give meaning to the phrase, 'It's the thought that counts'.

Many of the ideas are grouped together in the form of 'theme baskets', so that you can make a collection of co-ordinated items as a composite present, or choose to create a single gift as a smaller token.

DECORATIVE BASKETS

A BASKET OF shiny evergreens spiced up with cinnamon quills and rosy apples, pine-cones and berry-red flowers; a cone-encrusted basket arranged with an equally arresting green and scarlet theme, or one with an imaginative combination of brilliant red peppers and the most colourful blooms around – who could resist baskets like these? They serve as ready-made Christmas decorations and make thoughtful presents for a busy host or hostess, or for a friend who may not have ready access to a selection of seasonal greenery.

Choose the basket with special care. It forms an important part of the gift, since it will remain as a functional memento long after the flowers and foliage have faded. A suitable idea might be a shallow rectangular Shaker basket made from wide, woven slats. It looks beautiful simply piled with cones or apples; lined with checked napkins holding muffins or bread rolls; or laden with cookies and cakes to take to a bring-a-dish party.

BASKET OF EVERGREENS

All things bright and beautiful and appropriate to the Christmas season are here in this cheerful gift basket. Tartan ribbons on the handle bring together the red and green of the contents.

EQUIPMENT
* florists' adhesive clay
* 2 plastic prongs
* shallow rectangular basket
* 2 pieces absorbent stem-holding foam, soaked in water
* foil
* medium stub wires (floral pins)

DECORATIVE MATERIALS
* selection of evergreens such as holly, ivy, yew, cypress and spruce
* red spray carnations
* Christmas roses
* dried poppy seedheads
* pine-cones
* fruits such as pineapples, apples and grapes
* cinnamon quills

LEFT: Cut the top from a red pepper, fill the cavity with soaked absorbent stem-holding foam and you have a brilliant container for vivid flowers.

1 Press a piece of florists' clay to the underside of each plastic prong and press them in position, one on each side towards the back of the basket. Wrap the two pieces of foam in the foil and press each onto a prong.

2 Position sprays of evergreen to fan out over the four corners of the basket, so that neighbouring textures and foliage shapes contrast as much as possible. Arrange the spray carnations, poppy seedheads, and Christmas roses against the background of foliage.

VIVID CONTRAST

For a gift that is out of the ordinary, contrast the rugged look of a basket covered with pine-cones with the delicate beauty of rosebuds and freesias. You can cover any sturdy basket with pine-, larch- or other cones, using a hot glue gun and pressing them firmly onto the surface for a few seconds until they are fixed.

1 Cut two or three short lengths of florists' clay and press them to the underside of the plastic saucer. Insert the foam in the saucer and place the saucer in the basket.

2 Cut short sprays of the evergreen and arrange them to follow the shape of the basket, with the tallest stems just reaching the handle. Position the roses to follow the outline created by the foliage, with tall stems near the handle and short ones around the rim.

3 Fill the arrangement with the freesias, placing some so that they face out to either side and, from the front, are seen in profile. Add a gift tag and, if you wish, a bright glass bauble.

4 Bright scarlet roses and glossy evergreens make the perfect colour combination.

EQUIPMENT

* florists' adhesive clay
* scissors
* plastic foam-holding saucer
* cylinder of absorbent stem-holding foam, soaked in water
* cone-covered basket
* florists' scissors

DECORATIVE MATERIALS

* evergreen leaves such as escallonia or variegated holly
* red rosebuds
* cerise freesias

3 Twist stub wires around the lowest row of 'petals' in the pine-cones. Twist the ends together beneath the cones, and push the false stems into the foam.

4 Arrange the fruit to fill the basket; it should have a generous look. Tie ribbon bows around the handle on each side. The arrangement would look good in a hallway or a hearth, on a dining table or a sideboard.

Making Pot-pourri

Pot-pourri, an aromatic blend of dried flowers and petals, herbs and spices, was an essential part of the home environment in the Middle Ages, when it was made in large households to scent rooms and mask unwelcome odours. It was sewn into linen bags to hang in cupboards, displayed in large open bowls, packed into perforated holders and even scattered on the floor or the hearth. Centuries later, pot-pourri is making a strong comeback, appreciated now as much for the therapeutic joy of making it as for the endless permutations of colours, textures and aromas it offers.

There are two distinct ways of making it, known respectively as the moist and the dry methods. The moist method, the one with the longer pedigree, consists of layering partially dried flowers, petals and leaves in a moisture-proof lidded box (this must not be made of metal) with salt, which acts as a desiccant and draws out the natural moisture in the plant materials. The box is covered and set aside for ten days, after which the mixture will have fermented and formed a solid block. This is broken up, placed in a jar or crock and blended with powdered spices such as cinnamon, allspice, cloves, mace and nutmeg, and with a fixative such as ground orris-root powder or gum benzoin. It is then set aside, except for daily stirring, for six weeks. A few drops of an essential plant oil such as attar of roses may then be added to enhance the aroma. After a further two weeks the pot-pourri will be ready for use.

Spicy Orange Pot-pourri

Dry method

25g/1oz coriander seeds
25g/1oz whole cloves
50g/2oz star anise
15g/½oz cinnamon bark, crumbled
15g/½oz allspice berries
dried rind of 2 oranges, crumbled
1 tbsp ground cinnamon
1 tbsp ground orris-root powder

Mix all the ingredients together and set them aside in a lidded container for four weeks, stirring daily to blend the aromas.

Rose Petal and Lavender Pot-pourri

Dry method

2 cups dried rose petals
1 cup dried lavender flowers
1 cup dried herb leaves such as pineapple mint, thyme, lemon verbena
1 tbsp ground cinnamon
1 tbsp ground allspice
2 tbsp ground orris-root powder
2 drops lavender oil

Mix ingredients as for Spicy Orange Pot-pourri.

OPPOSITE: To make pot-pourri by the moist method, partially dried petals and small flowers are layered in a shallow dish with salt, which acts as a desiccant and draws out the moisture. Rose petals, marigold petals and larkspur (delphinium) flowers make a colourful blend.

Dry Pot-pourri

Pot-pourri made by the dry method is a blend of pre-dried flowers, petals and leaves with the ground spices, fixatives and oils mentioned above. To make pot-pourri in this way you can dry plant materials over an extended period and spanning several seasons, or use dried-flower off-cuts from your collection.

Pot-pourri recipes are infinitely variable and you can compose mixtures biased towards sweet, citrus or pungent aromas to suit your personal preference. As a general guide, to every 4 cups of dried plant material allow 2–3tbsp powdered spices, 2tbsp ground orris-root powder or other fixative, a strip of dried citrus fruit peel, and 2 drops of an essential oil. Place the dried plant materials, spices and fixative in a lidded container and stir them daily with a spoon or with your fingers – the therapeutic part of the process – for six weeks. Add the oil and set aside, stirring every day or two, for another two weeks.

POT-POURRI POWER

A dried-flower arrangement with the lasting aroma of pot-pourri – give as a gift, or give the components for the recipient to make themselves.

1 Cut the foam to fit the container, leaving a gap of 1.5cm/½in all round, and extending about 2.5cm/1in above the container. Place a piece of adhesive clay on the bottom of each prong; set the prongs in the container, and position the foam securely on top of the prongs.

2 Spoon the pot-pourri mixture into the gaps on all sides, and to conceal all but the top of the foam. Position the selection of dried flowers and herbs throughout the foam, ensuring that the design is well-rounded, and does not present a flat plane with the front of the container.

EQUIPMENT
* glass container
* scissors
* dry stem-holding foam
* florists' adhesive clay
* plastic prongs
* knife

DECORATIVE MATERIALS
* about 125g/6oz pot-pourri, depending on size of container
* selection of dried flowers and herbs, such as roses, carnations, peonies, statice, cornflowers, marjoram and purple sage

ORCHID BLEND

DRY METHOD

This is a romantic and pretty way to preserve the
memory of a special gift of orchids or other luxury
flowers.

1 cup dried orchid flowers
1 cup dried carnation petals
1 cup dried peony petals
1 cup dried marjoram leaves
1tbsp ground ginger
1tsp ground cloves
2tbsp ground orris-root powder
2 drops carnation oil

Mix ingredients as for Spicy Orange Pot-pourri.

MARIGOLD MIXTURE

MOIST METHOD

2 cups partially-dried rose petals
1 cup partially-dried marigold petals
1 cup partially-dried larkspur (delphinium) flowers
about 50g/2oz salt
1tbsp ground coriander
1tsp grated nutmeg
1tsp ground cloves
2tbsp ground orris-root powder
2 drops oil of cloves

*Mix the petals and salt, and leave in a moisture-proof lidded
box for 10 days. When the mixture has formed a solid block,
break up, and mix with the spices and orris-root powder.
Leave for 6 weeks, and add a few drops of essential oil. Leave
for another 2 weeks before using.*

*RIGHT: Rose Petal and
Lavender Pot-pourri (left) and
Marigold Mixture (right).*

POT-POURRI HOBBY BASKET

COMPOSING A Christmas gift basket for a friend or relation could be the start of something big by inspiring a new and absorbing hobby for the recipient. The basket shown here is filled with a selection of ingredients that could be combined to create a variety of aromatic pot-pourri blends, a 'scroll' of suggested recipes and a decorative rosebud pomander, scented with cloves in the traditional way. To complete the floral theme, there are jars of rose-petal jelly, decorated inside and out with more petals.

Other 'ingredients' baskets could be made up of the materials needed for a friend new to the art of flower arranging. This could include wires and scissors, with dried flowers for a decorative touch.

ROSE PETAL JELLY

Make the jelly in a similar way to the lavender jelly shown on the previous pages, using the same proportion of apples and sugar. In place of the lavender flowers, add a cup of scented rose petals such as those plucked from red or cerise damask roses. Wash the petals and pull off the white tips which can give a bitter flavour. Add another handful of rose petals when you boil the strained fruit juice and sugar and remove them before the preserve reaches setting point.

Make your gift as delightful to look at as it is to taste. Pour it into inexpensive glasses instead of preserve jars (warm them first) and press fresh rose petals onto the surface. Glue pressed petals to the glass and add a ribbon bow as a finishing touch.

LEFT: Packed in vibrant pink tissue paper with a scattering of rose petals, this gift basket has the makings of many an aromatic pot-pourri blend. It has decorative elements, too, a rosebud pomander, ribbon-tied glasses of preserve, and a dried full-blown peony.

ROSEBUD POMANDER

Encourage the recipient to get into the pot-pourri mode by including a pretty rosebud pomander.

EQUIPMENT

* 7.5cm/3in dry foam ball
* whole cloves
* dried rosebuds
* florists' scissors
* 1.5cm/¾in-wide bow
* scissors
* stub wires (floral pins)
* wire cutters

1 Stud the dry foam ball with cloves, to give the decoration the authentic aroma of a medieval pomander. Cut the rosebud stems to equal lengths, about 5cm/2in, and press them into the foam so that the flowers just touch.

2 Tie the ribbon into a bow. Bend half a stub wire to make a U-shaped staple, thread it through the back of the loop and press it into the foam.

3 If you have to keep the pomander any length of time before Christmas, put it in a bag with a few cloves and a crumbled cinnamon stick to retain and even intensify the aroma.

POT-POURRI HEART

Pour out your heartfelt feelings with a gift of a pretty pot-pourri heart. No-one would guess its humble beginnings!

1 Cut the foam block in half lengthways and stick the two halves together with hot glue. Draw the shape of the heart and cut it with a sharp knife. Working on small sections at a time, cover the top and sides with glue and press on the pot-pourri.

2 When the shape is covered, tie a bow with the unfurled paper ribbon and fix it to the heart with a bent stub wire. Stick a peony in place and stick the rose in its centre.

EQUIPMENT

* block of dry stem-holding foam
* hot glue gun
* pencil
* knife
* half stub wire

DECORATIVE MATERIALS

* pot-pourri, about 100g/4oz/ ½ cup
* dried peony
* dried rose

DELICIOUS GIFTS

TAKE A selection of fresh and dried fruits, dip them in chocolate or fondant (sugarpaste) and transform them into colourful and delectable *petits fours*. For the prettiest effect, only partially cover the fruit so that you have an irresistible visual combination – the contrasting textures and colours of the fruit and the sweet coating.

You can use almost any firm fruits of your choice, with strawberries perhaps making the prettiest presentation. Dip them chevron style, first into the bitter chocolate and then, when that has set, in white chocolate for a dramatic three-colour effect. Other delicious possibilities are fresh dates, pitted and filled with marzipan; kumquats, which look like sugar-coated acorns; orange and tangerine segments; cherries; and Cape gooseberries (physalis) released from their papery cases.

Among dried fruits you can choose prunes, dramatic when coated with either white chocolate or fondant (sugarpaste); apricots; semi-dried figs (do not use the sugar compressed ones in this way); and whole dates.

Crystallized (candied) fruits such as orange segments and mango slices can be enhanced with a chocolate coating. Covering them with fondant (sugarpaste) may seem, in terms of sweetness, like gilding the lily.

ABOVE: Make the wrappings as stylish as the contents for an irresistible gift. This box is wrapped in gold paper and tied with a black and gold ribbon.

RIGHT: Prunes dipped in pink fondant (sugarpaste), and fresh dates dipped in green make a colourful combination.

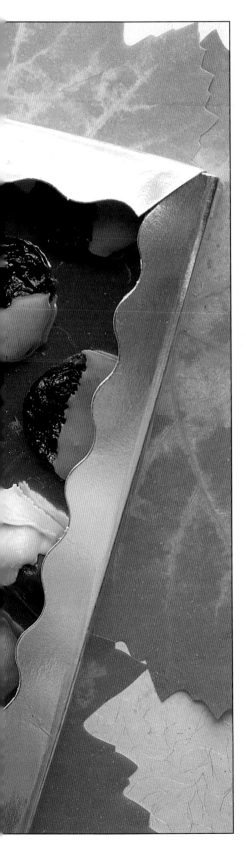

CHOCOLATE COATING

Use a good quality Swiss or Belgian chocolate when making home-made treats.

1 Melt bitter (semi-sweet) chocolate and white chocolate separately in bowls over a pan of simmering water. Do not allow the water to reach the bowl, or the chocolate may overheat.

2 Holding each piece of fruit on a toothpick, partially dip it in the chocolate. Place the fruits in rows on non-stick baking paper and leave them in a dry place – not a hot, steamy kitchen – to set. Dried crystallized (candied) fruit will keep well for several weeks in an airtight container. Fresh fruits will last only for their normal shelf life.

LEFT: Kumquats in green fondant (sugarpaste) take on the shape of acorns. The tanginess of the fruit contrasts well with the sweet covering.

QUINCE PASTE

This is known in Spain as *pasta de membrillo*, where it is decorated with icing sugar and sometimes cloves, and served after meals or to garnish desserts. To pack the paste as a gift, layer it in a box between sheets of non-stick baking paper.

INGREDIENTS
1kg/2¼lb quinces
1 litre/1¾pt/4⅓ cups water
1kg/2¼lb/4¼ cups sugar
vegetable oil, for brushing
icing (confectioners') sugar, for dusting
whole cloves, to garnish

1 Wash and slice the quinces and put them into a large pan with the water. Bring to the boil, then simmer for about 45 minutes, until the fruit is soft.

2 Mash the fruit against the sides of the pan, then spoon it and the liquid into a jelly bag suspended over a large bowl. Leave to drain for at least 2 hours, without squeezing the bag.

3 Pour the strained juice into the cleaned pan, add the sugar and stir over a low heat to dissolve. Cook over a low heat for about 2 hours, stirring frequently, until a spoon drawn through the paste parts it into 2 sections.

4 Lightly brush a Swiss roll tin (jelly roll pan) with oil, pour in the preserve and leave to set. When it is cool, cut it into diamonds or other shapes, brush with icing sugar and stud each piece with a clove. Store between layers of non-stick baking paper in an airtight container.

Makes about 1.25kg/2½lb

TURKISH DELIGHT

INGREDIENTS
300ml/½pt/1¼ cups hot water
25g/1oz/1tbsp powdered gelatine
450g/1lb/2 cups sugar
scant ½tsp citric acid
130ml/2tbsp rosewater
50g/2oz/¼ cup icing (confectioners') sugar
25g/1oz/1tbsp cornflour (cornstarch)

1 Pour the water into a pan, sprinkle on the gelatine and stir in the sugar and citric acid. Stir over a low heat until the sugar dissolves. Bring to the boil, and boil for 20 minutes. Remove the pan from the heat and set aside for 10 minutes without stirring. Stir in the rosewater.

2 Rinse a Swiss roll tin (jelly roll pan) in cold water, then pour in the mixture. Level the top and leave in a refrigerator for 24 hours.

3 Sift together the icing sugar and cornflour and sprinkle on a piece of non-stick baking paper. Turn the sweetmeat onto the paper and cut into squares with a sharp knife. Toss the pieces in the sugar mixture to coat them on all sides. Pack the pieces between layers of non-stick baking paper and store in an airtight container.

Makes about 600g/1¼lb

OPPOSITE: Tangy Quince Paste.

ABOVE LEFT AND BELOW: Turkish Delight.

CHRISTMAS CARDS AND WRAPPING

Take the most utilitarian brown wrapping papers and you can give them a new life with the luxury look of burnished gold. Sheets of coloured tissue can be transformed into gift wrappings that would seem fit for a king to open. Take a few pieces of card (posterboard) and scraps cut from used greetings cards and shape them into stylish and matching gift tags. Trace a traditional outline from a Christmas card onto embroidery cloth and sew greetings cards of your own. Look at the following suggestions for wrappings, cards and trims and let your creative ideas flow.

CUSTOMIZED TISSUE PAPER

Tissue paper is relatively inexpensive, readily available and it comes in a spectrum of colours, but it is undeniably plain. With a can or two of spray-paint you can soon alter that, creating fantastic all-over patterns that take plain ordinary tissue paper into the luxury class. Crêpe paper, another familiar yet unexciting wrapping, can be treated in similar ways – with style.

THE TIE-DYE TECHNIQUE

The technique used to dye fabrics with exotic sunburst designs can be adapted to give tissue and crêpe paper a colourful face-lift. Scrunch up small areas of the paper into a series of tight peaks (there is no need to use rubber bands, as with fabric) and spray over them with gold, silver or another colour. Repeat the process at intervals across the whole sheet of paper – the closer together the peaks, the more sunburst patterns will result. Leave the paper to dry, then open out the scrunches to reveal a series of shimmering patterns.

LEFT: Wrap a bottle in stiff card to make a neat cylinder and then wrap in tie-dyed tissue paper secured with double-sided adhesive tape. A band of pink-toning glitter ribbon and a cascading bow complete the trimmings.

ABOVE: Two special effects in process: tissue paper scrunched into peaks and sprayed with gold paint for a sunburst effect, and black crêpe paper crumpled into a ball for a crackled-metal finish.

RIGHT: Silver-sprayed black crêpe paper conceals a round Christmas pudding. The gift is placed in the centre of a square of decorated paper, the sides are drawn up over the pudding – the creases in the paper make this easier to do neatly – and tied around with silver thread. A design of fruit and leaves cut out of silver foil stuck onto a card makes a glittering tag.

For an even more metallic effect, scrunch up a sheet of paper into a ball and spatter-spray it with gold or silver. Allow the paint to dry for a few minutes, then turn the paper ball over and spray the other side. Allow it more time to dry, then open out the paper.

WRAPPING TIP

If you wish to restore tissue paper to its original, pristine and uncreased state you can place it on a sheet of plain paper and press it with a very cool iron on the unsprayed side. But this is not necessary. Creased paper which has been spray-painted has a certain style, and is much easier to wrap neatly around awkward parcel shapes such as spheres, and round or oval boxes.

RANDOM STRIPES

Tissue and crêpe paper patterned with gold and silver random stripes are equally dramatic, but in a completely different way. To achieve this gold-and-silver-dagger effect, cover a work surface or floor area with protective newspapers or scrap paper and place a piece of tissue paper or crêpe paper flat on top of it. The brighter or darker the colour of the paper to be decorated, the more outstanding the pattern will turn out to be.

Cut long, narrowly angled strips from newspaper or scrap paper and place them at random over the paper surface, angling them in any way you please. Secure the masking strips with double-sided adhesive tape, or hold them in place with the fingers of one hand.

Spray the unmasked areas of the tissue or crêpe paper with gold and silver paint so that the finished design will have a three-colour effect. Leave the paper to dry – you can hang it on a clothes line if you wish – and use the masking strips in random order to decorate other pieces of paper.

ABOVE: A boxed parcel shows off the striped paper to maximum effect. For added glamour, trim it with a double red and silver bow and glass baubles.

RIGHT: Tissue paper masked with randomly cut strips of newspaper is sprayed with gold and silver paints to create a dramatically modern look.

GIFT TAGS AND PLACE CARDS

MAKING YOUR own gift tags and place cards is an important part of pre-Christmas activity. You can not only save a significant sum of money by making these at home but also create a completely co-ordinated look for gift-wrapped presents and decorations. If you have chosen a particular colour scheme, especially if it is not a traditional one, you could spend fruitless time trying to buy the right shade and style of tags. By making these small but significant items yourself, you can be sure of making a perfect match.

Choose your wrapping paper first. It may be tissue paper, art paper with a marbled look, or crêpe paper scrunched into a ball and sprayed. Buy good-quality writing paper or plain postcards in appropriate colours for the gift tags. Look through any of last year's greetings cards you may have kept, and select motifs or panels to cut out. The used cards on these pages provided strips of gold for the abstract designs and the edgings, and a gold felt-tipped pen was used to outline some of the motifs.

LEFT: A golden bird motif cut from a used Christmas card decorates a plum-coloured gift tag. Gilded hydrangea florets echo the Midas look.

LEFT: *Traditional holly and bell shapes; abstract designs; motifs cut from used Christmas cards and gilded flower petals demonstrate the variety of designs that can be achieved with name tags created in a combination of three colours.*

LEFT: *Select cords and ribbons in colours and textures which harmonize or contrast with the cards. Both approaches are effective.*

ABOVE: *Horizontal place cards with a variety of motif decorations – a cut-out bird shape, a fresh pansy and a nursery-rhyme illustration. The napkin is wrapped with shiny cord in criss-cross formation.*

CINDERELLA STORY

TAKE THE most utilitarian and basic wrapping paper imaginable, plain brown parcel wrapping; take a can of gold spray-paint and a little imagination and you can achieve a design transformation of fairy-tale proportions.

THREE-DIMENSIONAL STENCILS

Use shapely leaves, nuts, shells, spices and other items from around the home as three-dimensional stencils. You could use a collection of varied items, some leaves, some shells, some nuts and so on, but using shapes of the same kind will give a more readable and recognizable pattern.

Cover a large, flat surface – a work table or even the floor – with newspaper or scrap paper and place a sheet of brown paper on it, right side up. Arrange a few of the 'stencils' either in rows or at random and using a can of gold spray-paint, spray lightly over the items. Leave them to dry partly for a minute or so, then move the stencils over the paper and spray over them again. Continue in this way until the paper is decorated all over. Leave it for about 30 minutes to dry. The completed design of gilded images makes wonderful wrapping paper.

ABOVE: A gold-stencilled brown paper parcel to the right of an evergreen arrangement forms part of a gold-accented still-life group.

RIGHT: Plain brown wrapping paper and a collection of natural stencils that could be used to decorate it. Leaves, nuts, shells and spices offer a wide variety of pattern shapes.

ABOVE: A dried fern with its intricate ladder-like outline makes an attractive 'stencil' when it is sprayed with gold paint.

RIGHT: Three parcels wrapped in gold-sprayed brown paper have a touch of class and individuality in the trims. A gingerbread tree dusted with gold powder and with false-berry candles tops a parcel that is tied around with red ribbon. Gilded hydrangea flowers add to the glitter and texture (top right). A stencil cut to a holly leaf shape and sprayed with gold makes the central feature of this parcel. The theme is echoed in the gold-sprayed holly leaf and the trim is completed with a raffia band (bottom). A length of gold beads becomes a parcel tie, with a pair of gold-sprayed vine leaves and a glittering star providing even more glamour (top left).

BELOW: A utilitarian brown paper bag undergoes a complete transformation when it is spatter-sprayed with both gold and silver paint. Here it is decorated with a trio of candies wired to the ribbon and with gilded hydrangea heads stuck onto one side.

EMBROIDERED CARDS

EMBROIDERED CHRISTMAS card designs are surprisingly simple to make, whether you are an embroidery enthusiast or have little or no experience with a needle, thread and canvas.

Card blanks with cut-out panels are available from hobby shops, or can be made at home. Cut a piece of stiff card (posterboard) to the required size. The cards illustrated on these pages range from 26 × 11cm/10½ × 4½in to 30 × 15cm/12 × 6in in size. Measure the card lengthways, divide it into three equal sections and fold it along the vertical lines. Cut a rectangular or oval panel from the centre section, which will become the frame for the embroidered design.

EMBROIDERED GIFT-WRAPPING

An embroidered stocking shape edged with red velvet and backed with red cotton makes a delightful tree decoration, or a miniature surprise to be brought down the chimney on Christmas Eve. Small in stature it may be (the stocking measures 14cm/5½in from the top to the toe) but there is room enough for a galaxy of gifts. The toe is packed with wrapped candies and kumquats – scaled-down versions of the traditional orange – and a candy stick, a toy musical instrument and a miniature Christmas cracker peep enticingly over the top.

ABOVE: A plainly-wrapped parcel is transformed by the addition of a double bow in toning colours. An embroidered greetings card does double duty as a gift tag.

LEFT: Christmas cards can provide ideas and outlines for embroidery designs of all kinds.

Use Christmas cards as inspiration for simple motifs – trees, churches, a pair of holly leaves or perhaps a manger scene. Attractive composite designs might include a group of candles, a small galaxy of stars, a pair of bells – the possibilities are endless.

Transfer the design onto graph paper, where each square will represent one cross-stitch. Cut a piece of embroidery canvas with space to spare, and, if you wish, mark the design with felt-tipped pens in the appropriate colours. This simple expedient will prevent you having to count stitches or cross-refer to the graph-paper pattern and will save time.

Stitch the design in cross-stitch, using double embroidery thread, and outline it in black, if desired. The holly and manger designs were both emphasized in this way. When the design is complete, cut the canvas slightly larger than the open panel and stick it, face outwards, onto the back of the panel. Fold over the left-hand section of the card and stick it to cover the back of the canvas. A seasonal message can then be written on the inside of the card.

ABOVE: Four Christmas cards embroidered with seasonal motifs, from a sprig of holly with bright red berries to a church with colourful stained-glass windows.

59

MAKING CHRISTMAS CARDS

Making your own Christmas cards can be an absorbing project to occupy family members of all ages through many a long winter evening. Hand-made cards convey a more personal and meaningful message than bought cards ever can, and when the children become involved, the cards become even more precious. Cards such as these are destined to be pasted lovingly into a family memento album.

STENCILLED CARD

The Christmas tree card is made from a simple stencil and painted in three seasonal colours, green, red and gold. You can trace an outline from an old Christmas card, or draw it freehand. Symmetry of line and branch is not important. Children should not use a sharp craft knife to cut the stencil.

1 Cut plain card (posterboard) to make the Christmas card blanks. Fold the cards in half along the long sides. Trace or draw the tree outline onto a small piece of card (posterboard) and cut out the shape with a craft knife.

2 Dampen a sponge and dip it into green paint. Place the stencil centrally on the front of the card blank and dab on the green paint. It is more effective if the paint is not applied too evenly. Colour the rest of the cards and leave to dry.

3 With a small paintbrush and red paint, fill in the outline for the tree trunk and pot, and paint shapes to represent bells hanging on the tree branches. Wash the brush and paint gold stars on the tree shape and a crescent moon or star above it.

CUT-OUT MANGER CARD

Children can help by tracing the template outline on the card blanks, but the design itself should be cut out by adults or older children.

EQUIPMENT

* stiff card (posterboard)
* pencil
* ruler
* tracing paper
* craft knife
* envelopes
* silver felt-tipped pen

1 *Cut the card blanks to measure 19 × 13.5cm/7½ × 5¼in. Measure the centre along the 2 long edges and draw a thin pencil line from top to bottom. Measure the centre of both the left-hand and right-hand sections and draw thin pencil vertical lines. The card will now be marked into 4 equal sections. Trace the outline of the cut-out section from the template. Place the tracing in the centre section of the card, with the base of the tracing 4.5cm/1¾in from the base of the card. Draw over the traced outline onto the card.*

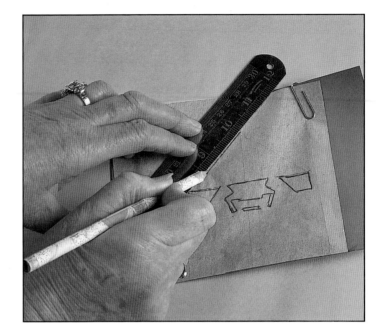

2 *Using the craft knife, cut around the imprinted outlines on the card. As the shapes are cut out, the outline of the Holy Family in the manger will appear. Measure and mark a point on the centre line 4cm/1½in above the top of the cut-out. This will form the roof of the manger. Draw a thin pencil line from this point to the top of the cut-out section on each side.*

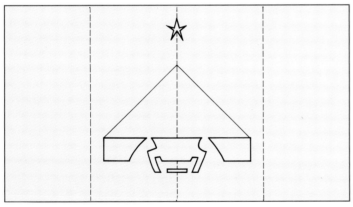

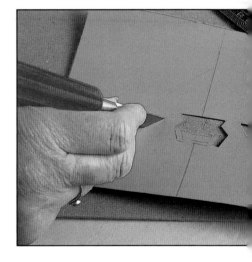

3 *To construct the manger, fold the 2 outside lines inwards to the centre. Fold the top and the bottom sections of the centre line in the opposite direction. The card will now fold into a long narrow strip. Fold the 2 diagonal lines marking the stable roof outwards and the centre line between them inwards.*

CHILDREN'S CHRISTMAS

Probably nothing can quite match the joy and excitement that children feel as Christmas approaches. This section of the book is designed to turn that excitement into creative energy, with projects for the children to make themselves. There are fully illustrated step-by-step instructions for gingerbread house biscuits (cookies), popcorn and candy garlands, table decorations and tree trims; projects for younger children to create bright and beautiful paper flowers and for older ones to cut out stained-glass patterns from card (posterboard) and tissue paper. All the projects are simple to make, and are certain to appeal to children of all ages.

DECORATING WITH CANDIES

LIGHT-AS-AIR and irresistible popcorn and brightly-wrapped candies come together to make the tastiest decorations ever. Let the children string popcorn and candies onto a thread to make garlands for the tree or to loop from side to side on a wall. Thread popcorn onto flexible wires to make pretty loops tied onto the tree branches with bright lengths of ribbon. And combine wired popcorn and threaded candies with two-colour holly leaves for a children's party centre-piece. They really are sweet ideas!

ABOVE: Seek out the candies with the brightest wrappings you can find, the shinier the better, and thread them onto double-thickness sewing thread. Take the needle through the candies for the long strips, through one end of the wrapping papers for the bunches at the side.

ABOVE: A wooden toy train can be used as the base of a flower arrangement for a children's party. Fix a plastic foam-holding saucer on the top, insert a cylinder of absorbent foam soaked in water and arrange a flurry of brightly coloured flowers and dried or evergreen leaves. The orange gerbera, like a giant daisy, has special child-appeal rivalled only by the toffee apples.

LEFT: A garland of candies and popcorn is a pretty and unusual tree trim that is becoming increasingly popular.

POPCORN AND CANDY RING

This is a design that older children can make by themselves, as a party centre-piece. Younger ones will need help in cutting the stub wires.

EQUIPMENT
* stub wires (floral pins)
* wire cutters
* 20cm/8in diameter pre-formed dry foam ring

DECORATIVE MATERIALS
* popcorn
* brightly wrapped candies
* variegated holly, or other evergreens such as ivy, cypress or pine
* 5cm/2in-wide ribbon

1 Cut the stub wires in half. Thread popcorn onto the wires to within 2.5cm/1in of the end. Push the threaded wires into the foam ring well spaced out all around. Bend some of the wires so that they face different ways.

2 Push a half-wire through one end of the candy wrapping, but not through the candy. Bend the ends of the wire downwards to make a U-shape, and twist the ends together.

3 Push the wired candies into the ring, mixing the colours and arranging the candies so that some face inwards and others outwards. Cut the holly or other evergreens into short sprays and press them into the foam ring to fill the gaps.

4 Tie the ribbon into a bow and thread a wire through the loop at the back. Twist the wire ends together and press it into the ring. Be sure to tell your guests that the candies are not for eating until after the party!

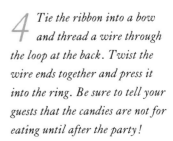

BRIGHT AND BEAUTIFUL

CHILDREN LOVE all things bright and beautiful, especially at Christmastime, when they are asked to play their part in decorating the home. Give them a specific project, beyond their naturally enthusiastic involvement in trimming the tree. It may be a garland made from threaded popcorn and candies; a group of pine-scented Christmas-tree candles, which older children could manage safely or a dish of Christmas-pudding-shaped candles ringed around at a safe distance with sprays of red-berried holly. Children will also enjoy making the following papercraft ideas created with jewel-bright tissue paper and paper glue.

PAPER FLOWERS

When bright colours are the order of the day realism is not important, as the paper flowers shown here demonstrate. Each petal is made of two circles of paper, folded, twisted into a cone and then glued edge-to-edge to its neighbour.

EQUIPMENT

* saucer or bowl 10cm/4in in diameter, or a pair of compasses
* pencil
* paper scissors
* paper glue

DECORATIVE MATERIALS

* tissue paper in various colours such as lime green, dark green and bright red

FOR A VASE OF FLOWERS

* narrow canes or strong wheat stalks
* jug or other tall container

FOR A GARLAND

* darning needle
* fine twine or strong thread
* 5cm/2in-wide ribbons (optional)
* 1 stub wire (floral pin), cut in half (optional)

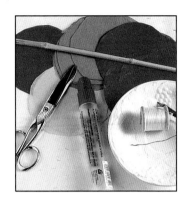

1. Trace around the saucer or bowl (or use the compasses) and cut out a number of 10cm /4in-circles in 3 colours of tissue paper. Make some flowers in a single colour and others in all 3 shades. Each flower needs about 14 petals, each one cut from 2 thicknesses of tissue paper. Taking 1 double circle, fold it once into a semicircle and again into quarters.

2 *Holding the paper shape by the point, between the thumb and first finger of one hand, put your other thumb and first finger into the cone and twist it sharply to open it out. It should be tightly twisted at the base so that it holds its shape.*

3 *When you have made several petals, stick them together by gluing along the length of one petal, from top to bottom, and pressing it to another one. Hold the joined edges for a few seconds while the glue sets. Continue gluing more and more petals to make a ball shape. Eventually, when you have come full circle, you will be gluing the first petal to the last one.*

4 *To make a vase of flowers, push a cane into the centre of each flower. If it does not stay firm, spread glue inside the lowest petal and wrap it around the stick. Arrange the flowers in a jug or other container and stand them in a place of honour. They make a lovely welcoming group in a hall or a bright feature in a room corner.*

5 *To make the garland, thread a darning needle with fine twine or strong thread and string the flowers together, mixing the colours as much as possible. If you wish, you can finish the design with ribbon bows at each end. To do this, push half a stub wire (floral pin) through the loop at the back, bend it to make a hook, and hook it over the garland.*

NEW-LOOK BAUBLES (GLASS BALLS)

Give the children a few plain baubles from last year's tree-trim box, a tube or two of glitter glue and a free hand in the design. They may come up with some works of art.

Encourage them to go for snappy colour contrasts – silver on red and deep pink baubles, red on silver ones, gold on dark green and so on.

Squiggle designs are interesting and fun, though the children's artistic flights of fancy may take in funny faces, names and seasonal messages.

'STAINED GLASS' PAPERCRAFT

Take a lead from the craftsmen and women who create wonderful patterns in stained glass and try your hand at this brilliant form of papercraft. Use black paper for the outlines and coloured tissue paper to fill in the shapes. Apart from that, all you need is a pair of paper scissors, a tube of paper glue and a little patience.

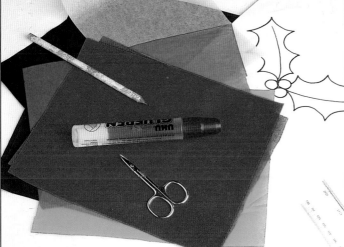

EQUIPMENT

* tracing paper
* pencil or ball-point pen
* ruler
* paper scissors
* paper glue
* patterns

DECORATIVE MATERIALS

* black art paper
* coloured tissue papers

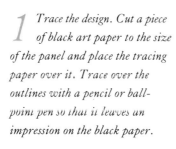

1 Trace the design. Cut a piece of black art paper to the size of the panel and place the tracing paper over it. Trace over the outlines with a pencil or ball-point pen so that it leaves an impression on the black paper.

2 Look at the finished designs in the photograph as a guide to the shapes which are to be cut out of the black paper and which ones will remain, to represent the leading in the window panels. Mark the areas to be cut out with a pencil or pen and cut around the outlines.

3 Cut tissue paper in the appropriate colours a little larger than the spaces which will be covered. Place it on the back of the black card design and draw the shape on the tissue paper, allowing a narrow overlap all round. Cut out the tissue paper and stick each piece on the back of the black panel, over the appropriate cut-out shape.

4 The candle panels are designed to be wrapped around straight-sided tumblers, or you could make them to decorate preserve jars. You can use any colourful tissue paper scraps you have, in any order. The candle flames are made in 2 colours, pale orange and red, for variety.

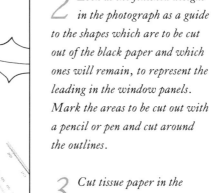

5 Make the candle panels to fit tumblers or preserve jars. Put a nightlight inside each one, and you have brilliant tablelamps that will be the stars of your Christmas party.

6 When the lights are turned down low the lamps look even more dramatic.

GINGERBREAD TREATS

YOUNG COOKS love to make treats that can be used to decorate the Christmas tree, become the centre of attraction on a party table, or be given as delicious take-home gifts to visitors of all ages. These gingerbread house biscuits (cookies) meet all these demands, and more.

The house shapes can be decorated in any way the young cooks like, with plain white and coloured icing to outline the roofs, doors and windows; and small coloured candies. They should be wrapped in transparent paper or plastic wrap if they are intended as gifts.

One batch of the mixture makes two house-shaped cookies and about 20 small shapes to trim the tree.

GINGERBREAD HOUSES

If these houses are to be given as gifts, write the name or house number of the recipient in icing.

INGREDIENTS
225g/8oz/2 cups plain (all-purpose) flour, plus extra for dusting
pinch of salt
1tsp baking powder
2tsp ground ginger
¹/2tsp ground cinnamon
125g/5oz/¹/2 cup unsalted butter at room temperature, cut into small pieces, plus extra for greasing
100g/4oz/¹/2 cup caster (superfine) sugar
2tbsp golden (dark corn) syrup
1 small egg, beaten, to mix

DECORATION
50g/2oz/¹/2 cup icing (confectioners') sugar
about 2tsp water or lemon juice
2–3 drops edible food colouring (optional)
chocolate drops and candies (optional)

LEFT: Stars, Christmas trees, hearts and other shapes cut out with cookie cutters and decorated with icing make pretty tree ornaments.

EQUIPMENT
* weighing scales
* large spoon
* teaspoon
* sieve (sifter)
* mixing bowl
* cup or small bowl
* fork
* pastry board
* plastic bag
* piece of white stiff card (posterboard)
* ruler
* pencil
* rolling pin
* knife
* spatula
* baking sheet
* small bowl
* icing bag
* small plain icing nozzle to pipe lines

DECORATIVE MATERIALS
* star-, tree- and heart-shaped biscuit (cookie) cutters
* skewer
* wooden toothpick
* small icing nozzle to pipe stars
* narrow ribbon or cord for hanging

1 *Sift together the flour, salt, baking powder, ground ginger and ground cinnamon into the mixing bowl. You will have to do this in several batches. Using your fingertips, rub in the butter until the mixture looks like breadcrumbs. Add the sugar and golden (dark corn) syrup and mix it well. Add just enough of the egg to make a stiff dough.*

2 *Sprinkle a little flour onto a pastry board, turn out the gingerbread dough and knead it with your hands until there are no more cracks. Put the ball of dough into a plastic bag and leave it in the refrigerator for about 30 minutes.*

3 *While the dough is chilling, make the template to cut out the house shapes. On a piece of white stiff card (posterboard), draw a rectangle 20 × 10cm/8 × 4in and cut it out. Measure and mark the centre of one of the short sides. Measure 7.5cm/3in down from the top on each long side and make marks. Draw lines from those marks to the centre top and cut along them. That represents the roof line.*

4 *Take out the dough. Sprinkle a little more flour onto the pastry board and roll out the dough until it is about 5mm/ 1/8in thick. Set the oven to 180°C/350°F/Gas 4.*

5 *Use the card template to make the house shapes, cutting round the outline with the points of a knife.* ▶

ABOVE: Gingerbread House cookies line up along the most exciting street ever. A slice of orange completes the picture.

6 Carefully, lift up the dough houses with a spatula and place them well apart on the baking sheet.

7 Using the cookie cutters, cut out star, heart and other shapes from the rest of the dough. Gather up the pieces left over, roll them into a ball, sprinkle a little more flour onto the pastry board and roll them out to the same thickness as before. Cut out as many shapes as you can. Push a hole near the top of each with the skewer and lift them onto the baking sheet.

8 Bake the gingerbread in the oven for 12–15 minutes, until it is pale golden brown and just beginning to darken at the edges. Take the baking sheet from the oven and leave the gingerbread to cool thoroughly on the sheet.

9 Use the spatula to transfer the shapes to the cleaned pastry board.

10 Sift the icing (confectioners') sugar into a small bowl, and add just enough water or lemon juice so that it makes a stiff paste when you mix it. If you want to add food colouring (an adult should help children with this) divide the mixture into two or three and add 1 drop of each colour to each. It is easiest to do this accurately by dipping a toothpick into the bottle of colouring, and shaking a drop off the end of it and into the bowl. Mix well, to achieve an even colour.

11 Put the plain nozzle into an icing bag, spoon some of the icing mixture into it and pipe the detail on the house shapes.

12 Use a little of the icing to stick chocolate drops or other candies to the house shapes, if you use them.

13 Wash the icing bag and put in the star nozzle. Pipe blobs of icing onto the star, tree and heart shapes. When it is dry thread narrow ribbon through the holes in the cookies to hang them on the tree.

RIGHT: A Gingerbread House cookie makes a lovely, if breakable, take-home present after a party. Wrap each one in cling film (plastic wrap) and tie it with pretty ribbons.

THE CHRISTMAS DINNER

For most, Christmas dinner is the meal of the year, and the one for which the host and hostess, family and friends reserve the highest hopes and the greatest of expectations. It is your privilege and responsibility to plan the preparation, cooking and presentation of the meal with meticulous precision, leaving nothing — not one tiny detail — to chance. Turn the page, study the multi-choice menu and weigh up the alternatives offered for each course. Once you have decided what to cook, as long as you follow the clear and concise instructions carefully, the preparation for the meal should be trouble-free.

THE FIRST COURSE

By the time the guests assemble around the table for the Christmas dinner, the scene is set for the feast that is to come. Their initial impressions – apart from tantalizing smells wafting in from the kitchen – will be visual. This is the moment when the guests will appreciate the care taken in setting the table – the sparkling glass, the polished cutlery, the flickering candles, and the festive flowers.

The first course should be a continuation of this visual feast, a dish that looks both appetizing and attractive, but which is not going to be too filling.

Following these suggestions, the recipes below are for a Melon Basket filled with melon balls and cranberries tossed in vodka, and for Gravad Lax, or Gravlax, the freshest of salmon fillets marinated in salt, herbs and spices.

You can prepare the Melon Basket on Christmas Eve; wrap it in plastic wrap or foil and keep it in the refrigerator, while the melon and cranberry mixture, stored in a lidded container, has time for the flavours to blend and mellow.

The Gravad Lax, should be prepared two or at the most three days ahead of serving.

MELON AND CRANBERRY BASKET

INGREDIENTS
1 large ripe cantaloupe melon
150g/6oz/1 cup fresh or frozen cranberries
4tbsp water
50g/2oz/¼ cup granulated sugar
4tbsp vodka
caster (superfine) sugar, to taste, if needed
scented geranium leaves, threaded cranberries or flowers to decorate (optional)

1 Cut the melon as illustrated, scoop out the flesh in balls and place it in a lidded container.

2 Put the cranberries, water and granulated sugar into a small pan, bring slowly to the boil, stirring from time to time, and simmer until the fruit is just tender but not bursting. Remove the pan from the heat and set aside to cool. Remove the cranberries with a draining spoon and add them to the melon balls. Stir in the vodka, cover and chill.

3 Pile the fruit mixture into the melon basket and decorate with scented geranium leaves, with a string of threaded cranberries or flowers, as you wish. Serve chilled.

Serves 6

CUTTING A MELON BASKET

1 Draw a faint line around the melon, about ⅔ of the way from the base. Draw two parallel lines from side to side, about 2cm/¾in apart, over the top of the melon and down to the line on each side. These form the outline of a handle. Cut a small slice from the base of the melon, so that it stands firmly.

2 With a sharp knife, cut along the two lines to form the handle.

3 With the point of the knife, make a diagonal cut through the sides of the melon, just below the drawn line. Remove the knife and insert it at right angles to the first cut, to make a point. Continue in this way all round the melon.

LEFT: Melon and Cranberry Basket makes a refreshing and light first course.

4 Using a curved knife, cut
away the melon flesh,
taking care not to cut through the
skin. Scrape away the seeds.

5 With a melon baller or
teaspoon, scoop out rounds
of melon as close to each other as
possible.

6 Use the shell and melon
balls for the Melon and
Cranberry Basket opposite, or
add other seasonal fruit of your
choice.

MUSTARD SAUCE

INGREDIENTS

½tsp white wine vinegar
1tbsp clear honey
1tsp French mustard
freshly ground black pepper
150ml/¼pt/⅔ cup sour cream

Mix together the vinegar, honey
and mustard and season with
pepper. Gradually stir in the
sour cream and beat until the
sauce is smooth. Serve chilled.

Makes 175ml/5l/2fl oz/¾ cup

GRAVAD LAX

INGREDIENTS

fresh salmon, about 1.5kg/3¼lb
1 large bunch fresh dill or fennel
50g/2oz/¼ cup coarse salt
50g/2oz/¼ cup caster (superfine)
sugar
1tbsp dried dill seeds
2tbsp white or black peppercorns,
crushed
1tsp mustard seeds
1 or 2 small dried red chillies
(optional)
lemon wedges, to serve
cucumber slices, to serve

1 Buy the fish with the
backbone removed, cut in
half lengthways. Place one side of
the fish, skin-side down, in a
glass or enamel dish and place the
bunch of dill or fennel on it.

2 In a bowl, mix together the
salt, sugar, dill seeds,
peppercorns and mustard seeds.

3 Sprinkle the mixture evenly
over the fresh dill or fennel
and add the chillies if you use
them. Place the other salmon
fillet over the spices, with the
skin-side up.

4 Cover the fish with foil and
place a heavy dish over it.
Place some weights on the dish —
cans of food are suitable — and
chill in the refrigerator for 2 or
3 days. Turn the fish over every
12 hours, basting it inside and
out with the spiced brine that
accumulates. Replace the dish
and weights each time.

5 When you are ready to
serve the fish, remove it

from the dish, scrape off the herbs
and spices and pat it dry with
paper towels. Place the fish skin-
side down and slice it as thinly as
possible, cutting diagonally across
each fillet.

6 Garnish the fish with lemon
wedges and cucumber, and
serve it with Mustard Sauce.

Serves 8

ROAST TURKEY

TURKEY, THE joyous discovery of New World settlers in the seventeenth century, has since gained in popularity across the Western world as the prime festive offering. In the United States turkey is devoured with equal relish at Thanksgiving and then, scarcely a month later, on Christmas Day. In Britain this plump, intensively farmed bird has long replaced goose as the most popular Christmas Day fare; and as for the rest of Europe, turkey is gaining ground all the time. In Greece, for example, it now takes pride of place over the more traditional roast pork, and even in Germany it now frequently displaces goose on the Christmas table.

While there are, naturally, family and regional preferences for the various stuffings, sauces and vegetables which can accompany roast turkey, some are now so widely accepted that they have become closely woven into the tradition of serving the bird itself. Chestnut Stuffing, Cranberry Sauce – as much for its ruby-red translucence as for its tangy flavour – Brussels Sprouts with Chestnuts, and roast potatoes combine to further the enjoyment of the meal. These and other recipes are included below, along with thawing times, quantities of stuffings required and roasting times for birds of varying weights and sizes.

ROAST TURKEY

INGREDIENTS

1 oven-ready turkey, 4.5kg/10lb
2 types of stuffing (see recipes
on following pages)
100g/4oz/1/2 cup butter, softened
1/2 lemon
salt and freshly ground black
pepper

FOR THE GRAVY

giblets from the bird, if available,
washed (save the liver for
sausagemeat stuffing)
4 cloves
1 onion, skinned and quartered
2 stalks celery, sliced
1 carrot, sliced
1 tbsp plain (all-purpose) flour
600ml/1pt/2 1/2 cups water or
meat stock (see method)
3 tbsp dry white wine or cider

1 Remove the turkey from the refrigerator at least 3 hours before cooking. Heat the oven to 220°C/425°F/Gas 7.

2 Wipe the turkey inside and out with a damp cloth and dry it with paper towels. Pack the chosen stuffing in the bird, a different one at each end – it is usual to have the chestnut or sausagemeat stuffing at the tail end of the bird and a fruit or herb stuffing at the neck end.

3 Ease the skin away from the breast meat and rub in the softened butter. Rub the skin with the lemon and season with salt and pepper. Place the bird breast-side up on a wire rack in a roasting pan and cover it loosely with foil. Do not wrap tightly or the bird will steam rather than roast in the oven.

4 Place the pan in the oven. After 20 minutes, reduce the heat to 180°C/350°F/Gas 4 and continue cooking for a further 3 1/2 hours, basting the turkey with the fat and pan juices every 20 or 25 minutes.

5 Remove the foil, baste the turkey again and increase the oven temperature to 200°C/400°F/Gas 6. Continue cooking the bird to brown the skin for a further 30 minutes, or until the meat is well cooked. To test that the turkey is ready to serve, insert a fine skewer into the thickest part of one of the legs. The juices that run out should be clear and show no traces of pink.

6 Place the giblets in a pan. Stick the cloves into the onion and add to the pan with the celery and carrot. Pour on the water. If no giblets are available, use a meat stock or a stock cube. Slowly bring to the boil and, if giblets are used, skim off the foam that rises to the surface. Cover the pan and simmer for 1 hour.

7 When the turkey is cooked, transfer it to a warmed serving plate, cover it loosely with foil and keep it warm until ready to serve.

8 Pour off the fat from the turkey pan, reserving the juices. Stir in the flour over a low heat until it forms a roux. Strain the stock from the saucepan and gradually stir it into the roux. Add the wine or cider and stir until the gravy thickens and is smooth and glossy. Season to taste with salt and pepper. Serve hot.

Serves 10–12

ABOVE: Casual, yet elegant enough for the Christmas Dinner, ivy-green linen napkins are trimmed with variegated holly.

OPPOSITE: Roast turkey is garnished with glazed apricots and served with bacon rolls and small chestnut and sausagemeat balls, made from extra stuffing. The stuffings shown are Cranberry and Rice, Chestnut, and Apricot and Raisin. They are baked in ovenproof dishes for the last 30 minutes of the cooking time.

APRICOT AND RAISIN STUFFING

INGREDIENTS

40g/1¹/₂oz/3tbsp butter
1 large onion, sliced
100g/4oz/1 cup dried apricot
pieces, soaked and drained
100g/4oz/²/₃ cup seedless raisins
juice and grated rind of 1 orange
1 cooking apple, peeled, cored and
chopped
100g/4oz/2 cups fresh white
breadcrumbs
¹/₄tsp ground ginger
salt and freshly ground black
pepper

1 Heat the butter in a small
pan and fry the onion over
a moderate heat until it is
translucent.

2 Turn the onion into a bowl
and stir in the apricots,
raisins, orange juice and rind,
apple, breadcrumbs and ginger.

3 Season with salt and
pepper. Allow to cool, and
use to pack the neck end of the
bird.

Makes about 400g/14oz

CHESTNUT STUFFING

INGREDIENTS

40g/1¹/₂oz/3tbsp butter
1 large onion, chopped
450g/1lb can unsweetened chestnut
purée
50g/2oz/1 cup fresh white
breadcrumbs
3tbsp orange juice
grated nutmeg
¹/₂tsp caster (superfine) sugar
salt and freshly ground black
pepper

1 Heat the butter in a pan
and fry the onion over a
moderate heat for about 3
minutes until it is translucent.

*ABOVE: Three types of stuffing
before being cooked –
Cranberry and Rice,
Chestnut, Apricot and Raisin.
They may be cooked inside the
bird, in ovenproof dishes or as
forcemeat balls.*

2 Remove from the heat and
mix with the chestnut
purée, breadcrumbs, orange
juice, nutmeg and sugar.

3 Season with salt and
pepper. Allow to cool, and
use to pack the neck end of the
turkey.

Makes about 400g/14oz

CRANBERRY AND RICE STUFFING

INGREDIENTS

225g/8oz/1¼ cups long-grain rice, washed and drained
600ml/1pt/2½ cups meat or poultry stock
50g/2oz/4tbsp butter
1 large onion, chopped
150g/6oz/1 cup cranberries
4tbsp orange juice
1tbsp chopped parsley
2tsp chopped thyme
grated nutmeg
salt and freshly ground black pepper

1 Put the rice and stock into a small pan, bring to the boil and stir. Cover and simmer for 15 minutes, until the stock has been absorbed. Tip the rice into a bowl and set aside.

2 Heat the butter in a small pan and fry the onion until it is translucent. Add it to the rice in the bowl.

3 Put the cranberries and orange juice in the cleaned pan and simmer until the fruit is tender. Tip the fruit and any remaining juice into the rice.

4 Add the herbs and season to taste. Allow to cool, and use to pack the neck end of the turkey.

Makes about 450g/1lb

CRANBERRY MOULD

The mould may be refrigerated for 2–3 days, or frozen for up to 3 months.

INGREDIENTS

350g/12oz/2 cups cranberries, plus a few to decorate
2 large cooking apples, peeled, cored and chopped
100g/4oz/½ cup sugar
150ml/¼pt/⅔ cup dry cider
11g/scant ½oz/1tbsp gelatine crystals (1 sachet)
2tbsp water
leaves, to decorate

1 Put the cranberries, apples, sugar and cider into a pan and stir over a low heat until the sugar has dissolved. Bring to the boil and simmer, uncovered, for about 15 minutes, until the fruit is soft. Stir the fruit occasionally.

2 Meanwhile sprinkle the gelatine crystals onto the water in a small bowl or cup. Stand in a pan of hot water and stir occasionally to dissolve the crystals.

3 Purée the fruit mixture in a food processor or blender and stir in the gelatine mixture.

4 Pour the mixture into a wetted 900-ml/1½-pt/4-cup mould and chill for at least 3 hours.

5 To serve, run a knife around the edge and dip the mould briefly in hot water. Place a serving plate over the mould and, holding the two firmly together, invert it to release the jellied fruit. Decorate with fresh cranberries and leaves.

Serves 10–12

BELOW: Cranberry Mould, set in a copper mould, is garnished with fresh berries and leaves.

THAWING A FROZEN TURKEY

If you buy a frozen turkey, it is very important to make sure that it thaws thoroughly before cooking, so plan well ahead. In the case of a very large bird, you should buy it or remove it from the freezer 3–4 days in advance.

Remove the frozen turkey from any cardboard packaging, which would soon become sodden, and place it, still in the polythene bag, on a large dish. As it begins to thaw, remove the turkey from the bag, pour off the liquid and keep the bird covered with foil to prevent it from drying out.

THAWING TIMES FOR A FROZEN TURKEY

Weight	Thawed at room temperature (18°C/65°F) Hours	Thawed in refrigerator (4°C/40°F) Hours
2.5–3kg/5–6lb	18–20	40–50
3–3.5kg/6–8lb	20–23	50–60
3.5–4kg/8–10lb	23–26	60–66
4.5–5.5kg/10–12lb	26–29	66–70
5.5–7kg/12–15lb	29–31	70–74
7–8kg/15–17lb	31–33	74–78
8–9.5kg/17–20lb	33–35	78–82
9.5–11.5kg/20–25lb	35–40	82–86

STUFFING A TURKEY

The exact quantity of stuffing you will require will depend to some extent on the type of stuffing you choose and how closely you pack it into the bird. A light stuffing with a high proportion of breadcrumbs needs more space to swell than one with a dense consistency, such as sausagemeat stuffing.

As a general rule, 350g/12oz forcemeat (herb or fruit stuffing) and 350g/12oz sausagemeat stuffing will be enough to pack a turkey weighing 4.5kg/10lb. Any left-over stuffing can be cooked separately, in a well-greased dish covered with foil, for the last 30–45 minutes of the cooking time. Or you can shape forcemeat and sausagemeat into balls, shallow-fry them, and serve them hot or cold, with cold turkey, ham and other meats.

Always allow the stuffing to cool completely before using it to pack the bird; this is for sound health and hygiene reasons as warm stuffing packed into the bird is a breeding ground for dangerous bacteria. If you make stuffing in advance, store it in a lidded container in the refrigerator or freezer. Bring stuffing to room temperature before using it and pack the bird only just before cooking it. No matter how pressing the time schedule, do not stuff the bird the night before cooking.

QUANTITIES OF STUFFING

Weight of turkey	Total weight of stuffing
2.5–3kg/5–6lb	300–350g/10–12oz
3–3.5kg/6–8lb	350–450g/12oz–1lb
3.5–4.5kg/8–10lb	450–550g/1–1¼lb
4.5–5.5kg/10–12lb	550–700g/1¼–1½lb
5.5–7kg/12–15lb	700g–1kg/1½–2¼lb
7–8kg/15–17lb	1–1.25kg/2¼–2½lb
8–9.5kg/17–20lb	1.25–1.5kg/2½–3lb
9.5–11.5kg/20–25lb	1.5–2kg/3–4lb

PREPARING A TURKEY FOR THE OVEN

Once you have stuffed the turkey, perhaps with a savoury stuffing at the tail end and a fruit one at the neck end, truss the bird to give it a neat, compact shape and to prevent the stuffing from spilling out.

To do this, thread a special trussing needle or a large darning needle with fine twine. Place the bird breast-side down and bring the legs together to form a V-shape. Leaving a length of twine free for tying, insert the needle into one leg just above the thigh bone, pass it through the body and out through the other leg at a similar point. Turn the bird over and pass the thread through the central joint of the wing on each side. Twist the end of each wing under the neck to hold the flap of skin in place and tie the thread ends loosely together. Loop the thread over the ends of the legs and draw them together, tying the thread around the tail end.

ROASTING TIMES FOR A TURKEY

Weigh the turkey when it is stuffed and calculate the cooking time accordingly. Cook the bird for an initial 20 minutes at a high temperature, 220°C/425°F/Gas 7. Reduce the temperature to a moderate heat, 180°C/350°F/Gas 4, and continue cooking for the times below. If you decide to increase the oven temperature towards the end of the cooking time, to crisp and brown the skin a little more, reduce the cooking time by 10–15 minutes.

ROASTING TIMES

Weight	Hours
2.5–3kg/5–6lb	3–3½
3–3.5kg/6–8lb	3½–4
3.5–4.5kg/8–10lb	4–4½
4.5–5.5kg/10–12lb	4½–5
5.5–7kg/12–15lb	5–5½
7–8kg/15–17lb	5½–6
8–9.5kg/17–20lb	6–6½
9.5–11.5kg/20–25lb	6½–7½

CARVING THE TURKEY

It is customary to serve each guest with slices of breast meat and the dark meat carved from the legs, and the 'oysters', cut

from the shallow hollows between the thigh sockets.

To begin carving, insert the carving fork in the breast of the bird and make a firm, downward cut on each side between the thigh and the body. With the carving knife inserted at an angle or, somewhat easier, using poultry shears, cut through the bones to sever the legs. Leave them aside.

Now, with the fork still holding the bird steady, cut through the wings.

Carve the breast meat in large, thin, even slices, cutting from the breastbone down to the side of the carcass.

Carve the meat from the legs in thin slices, cutting downwards following the direction of the bone.

To serve the stuffing, slit the skin vertically down the centre at both ends. Turn back the skin and scoop out the stuffing with a spoon.

THE VEGETABLES

THE VEGETABLES accompanying the main dish have a very high standard to live up to and should be planned, timed and presented with equal care.

If you choose fresh vegetables, buy them as close to Christmas Day as possible, making them the last purchase on the shopping list. Buy them from an outlet which has a good reputation and a quick turn-over, and do not be afraid to scrutinize them carefully. Green vegetables such as Brussels sprouts and broccoli should be crisp and bright green. Limpness and yellowing are signs of age. Cauliflowers should be tightly closed and pure creamy-white. Dark patches or opened florets (flowerets) are tell-tale signs of lack of freshness. Root vegetables should be crisp and firm. Discoloured and limp leaves are the first signs of a fast-approaching sell-by date.

BRUSSELS SPROUTS AND CHESTNUTS

INGREDIENTS
1kg/2¼lb Brussels sprouts
about 450ml/¾pt/2 cups water or chicken stock
salt (optional)
25g/1oz/2tbsp butter
225g-/8oz-can chestnuts, rinsed and drained
freshly ground black pepper

1 Cut a slice from the base of each Brussels sprout, cut a cross in the base of large ones so that they cook evenly, and tear off the outer leaves.

2 Bring the water (salted, if you wish) or chicken stock to the boil in a pan, place a steamer over it, add the sprouts and cover. Steam over boiling liquid for 6–8 minutes, according to size, until the sprouts are just tender.

3 Melt the butter in a frying pan, add the sprouts and chestnuts and stir them carefully over a medium heat for 2–3 minutes. Transfer them to a warm serving dish, season with pepper, cover with foil and keep warm until ready to serve.

Serves 8

LEFT: Brussels Sprouts with Chestnuts and Caramelized Carrots and Onions make colourful vegetable dishes.

CARAMELIZED CARROTS AND BUTTON (PEARL) ONIONS

INGREDIENTS
750g/1½lb carrots, trimmed, scraped and cut into thin rings
225g/8oz button (pearl) onions, peeled
water to cover
salt
40g/1½oz butter
6tbsp chicken stock
1tbsp sugar
freshly ground black pepper

1 Put the carrots and onions into a pan, cover with salted water and bring to the boil over a high heat. Boil for 1 minute, then drain the vegetables.

2 Return them to the pan, add the butter, chicken stock and sugar and bring to the boil over a moderate heat, stirring occasionally. Cover the pan and simmer over a low heat for about 10 minutes until the vegetables have absorbed all the liquid and are glossy and dry.

3 Season with salt and pepper and transfer to a warm serving dish. Cover with foil and keep warm until ready to serve.

Serves 8

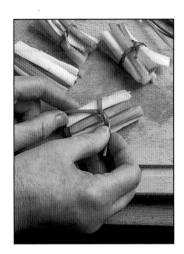

LEFT: *Vegetable Bundles of carrot, parsnip and celery are tied with chive leaves. Cauliflower florets and snap peas are arranged in the shape of a flower and decorated with a tomato rose.*

VEGETABLE BUNDLES

INGREDIENTS
450g/1lb carrots, trimmed and scrubbed
450g/1lb parsnips, trimmed and scrubbed
4 stalks celery, washed
about 450ml/3/4pt/2 cups water or chicken stock
salt (optional)
a few chive leaves
25g/1oz/2tbsp butter, melted

2 Remove the vegetables from the steamer and set them aside to cool.

3 Separate the vegetables into groups of 2 or 3 of a kind and tie them into bundles with chive leaves. You can prepare the vegetables to this point the day before you plan to serve them. In this case, cover them with plastic wrap and store them in the refrigerator.

4 To reheat the vegetables, steam them for 1–2 minutes over boiling liquid. Or cover them with plastic wrap and heat them in a microwave at full power for 1–1½ minutes. Arrange the vegetables on a heated serving dish and brush them with melted butter.

Serves 8

1 Cut the carrots, parsnips and celery into matchstick strips 7.5cm/3in long. (Reserve the trimmings to flavour soup.) Steam the vegetables over boiling, salted water or stock for 2–3 minutes, or until they are barely tender.

CAULIFLOWER AND PEA 'FLOWER'

INGREDIENTS
1 cauliflower, cut into florets (flowerets)
225g/8oz snap (edible pod) peas, trimmed or mange-tout (snow) peas
about 450ml/3/4pt/2 cups water or chicken stock
salt (optional)
1 firm tomato
15g/1/2oz/1tbsp butter, melted

1 Steam the cauliflower and peas over boiling salted water or stock for 5–7 minutes, until they are just tender.

2 Using a sharp knife or a rotary peeler, peel a long strip about 1.5cm/1/2in wide from the tomato. Coil the strip and pull up the centre to form the shape of a rose.

3 Remove the cauliflower and peas. Arrange the peas in a wheel pattern in the centre of a warmed serving dish. Arrange the cauliflower around the outside and place the tomato rose in the centre. Brush the vegetables with melted butter, cover the dish with foil and keep warm.

Serves 6–8

CHRISTMAS PUDDING AND MINCE PIES

FOR MANY people, this is the moment they have been waiting for; the moment when the lights are turned down low and the host or hostess brings in the Christmas pudding, wreathed in dramatic blue flames.

It is a matter of family custom whether the mince pies, are enjoyed at the same time as the pudding or as a second dessert course (in which case they must be kept warm or reheated, so that they will be hot enough to melt the traditional topping of rum or brandy butter).

It is also a matter of preference whether the 'hard sauce' is flavoured with one or other spirit – there will often be a no-alcohol version for the children – and whether there is custard sauce, creamy mousseline sauce or a slightly tipsy low-fat alternative.

CUMBERLAND RUM BUTTER

INGREDIENTS
225g/8oz/1 cup unsalted butter,
at room temperature
225g/8oz/1 cup soft light brown
sugar
6tbsp dark rum, or to taste

1 Beat the butter and sugar until the mixture is soft, creamy and pale in colour. Gradually add the rum almost drop by drop, beating to incorporate each addition before adding more. If you are too hasty in adding the rum, the mixture may curdle.

2 When all the rum has been added, spoon the mixture into a covered container and chill for at least 1 hour. It will keep well in the refrigerator for about 4 weeks.

Makes about 450g/1lb

RIGHT: In true Victorian tradition, a rich, dark and round Christmas pudding is decorated with a sprig of holly and flamed with brandy. A ruched ribbon around the base is a festive finishing touch.

ABOVE: Individual puddings make an attractive alternative presentation. Here they are ringed around and garnished with lightly poached cranberries.

MOUSSELINE SAUCE

INGREDIENTS
4 eggs
2 egg yolks
50g/2oz/¼ cup caster (superfine) sugar
150ml/¼pt/⅔ cup single (light) cream

1 Put all the ingredients in a double boiler or a bowl over a pan of simmering water. Do not allow the water to come into contact with the base of the bowl or upper pan.

2 Whisk until the mixture is pale and frothy. It should have a thick, creamy consistency. Serve at once.

Makes about 450ml/16floz

ORANGE BUTTER

This non-alcoholic sauce may be made for children, but it has many adult followers, too.

INGREDIENTS
100g/4oz/½ cup unsalted butter, at room temperature
100g/4oz/½ cup soft light brown sugar
grated rind of 2 oranges
juice of 1 orange

Make the sauce in a similar way to Cumberland Rum Butter, beating the orange rind with the butter and sugar and adding the orange juice gradually.

Makes about 225g/8oz

RIGHT: Mince pies decorated with holly-leaf shapes and dusted with icing (confectioners') sugar.

CUSTARD SAUCE

INGREDIENTS
4 eggs
75g/3oz/⅓ cup caster (superfine) sugar
150ml/¼pt/⅔ cup milk
300ml/½pt/⅔ cup single (light) cream
2 bay leaves

1 Beat together the eggs, sugar and milk. Beat in the cream and pour the mixture into a double boiler or a bowl over a pan of simmering water. Do not allow the water to come into contact with the base of the bowl.

2 Add the bay leaves and stir constantly with a wooden spoon for about 15 minutes, until the sauce thickens. Remove the bay leaves. Serve hot or cold.

Makes about 600ml/1pt

TIPSY YOGHURT

INGREDIENTS
4tbsp clear honey, plus extra for serving (optional)
3tbsp brandy
grated rind of 1 orange
300ml/½pt/1¼ cups Greek-style yoghurt

1 Stir the honey, brandy and orange rind until they are well blended, then gradually stir in the yoghurt.

2 Spoon the sauce into a covered container and chill in the refrigerator. If you wish, drizzle a little extra honey over the sauce an hour or so before serving. Transfer it to a serving dish before doing so.

Makes about 400ml/14floz

SPOILT FOR CHOICE

IF YOU wish to offer an alternative dessert for the Christmas meal, your guests will be spoilt for choice between refreshing Caramelized Oranges, Chocolate Meringue Yule Log, and Nesselrode Ice-cream.

CHOCOLATE MERINGUE YULE LOG

INGREDIENTS
6 eggs, separated
125g/5oz/²/₃ cup caster (superfine) sugar
50g/2oz/¹/₂ cup unsweetened cocoa powder, sifted
300ml/¹/₂pt/1¹/₄ cups double (heavy) cream, whipped

FOR THE TOPPING
2 egg whites
100g/4oz/¹/₂ cup caster (superfine) sugar
cranberries and holly leaves, to decorate (optional)

1 Heat the oven to 180°C/ 375°F/Gas 4. Line a Swiss roll tin (jelly roll pan) with non-stick baking paper.

2 Whisk the egg yolks until they are pale and creamy. Add the sugar and cocoa powder and continue whisking until the mixture thickens enough to hold its shape.

3 In a separate bowl, whisk the egg whites until they form soft peaks.

4 Spoon a little of the egg white into the cocoa mixture then carefully fold it into the remaining egg white.

5 Spread the mixture into the tin (pan). Bake in the oven for 20 minutes. Cool.

6 Sprinkle a little caster (superfine) sugar over a sheet of baking paper on a work surface. Invert the tin (pan) over the paper and shake it to release the cake. Peel off the paper from the base.

7 Spread the cream over the cake and roll it up from one long side. Cut a piece diagonally from one end. Place the main 'log' on a heat-proof dish and with the 'branch' at an angle.

8 For the topping, whisk the egg whites until they are stiff and glossy. Sprinkle on half the sugar and whisk until the meringue is stiff again. Fold in the remaining sugar.

9 Spread the meringue over the log to cover it completely. Return it to the oven for 6–7 minutes, until the meringue is pale brown. Allow the meringue to cool, then decorate it with cranberries and leaves, if you wish.

Serves 8

BELOW: *Caramelized Oranges, Chocolate Meringue Yule Log and Nesselrode Ice-cream.*

MARZIPAN
LOGS

INGREDIENTS

225g/8oz Marzipan, at room
temperature
100g/4oz/³/4 cup Candied orange
peel, chopped
2tbsp orange liqueur, or orange
juice
1tbsp golden granulated (light
brown) sugar
edible gold powder
75g/3oz bitter (semi-sweet)
chocolate, melted
gold-coated sweets (candies)

1 Knead the marzipan until
it is soft and pliable. Mix
in the chopped peel (it is easier to
do this with your fingers) and
gradually mix in the liqueur or
orange juice. Set aside for about
1 hour, to dry.

**LEFT: A selection of truffles
coated with white chocolate,
milk chocolate and bitter
(semi-sweet) chocolate.**

**ABOVE: Marzipan Logs. Some
are coated in bitter (semi-
sweet) chocolate, others dipped
in golden granulated sugar and
dusted with edible gold
powder.**

2 Break off small pieces of the
mixture, about the size of
pecan nuts, and roll them into
log shapes.

3 Dip the tops of half of the
marzipan logs in the sugar
and brush them lightly with
edible gold powder.

4 Dip the other half of the
logs in the melted chocolate
– it is easiest to do this if you
pierce them with a wooden
toothpick. Place the chocolate-
dipped logs on non-stick baking
paper and press a gold-coated
sweet (candy) in the centre of
each. When the logs are dry,
store them in a box in the
refrigerator. Bring them to room
temperature before serving.

CHRISTMAS BAKING

This chapter enables you to build on your own repertoire of Christmas specials, from a rich and fragrant pudding to spirit-soaked mincemeat, from fancy gingerbread men to moist gingerbread cake, both among the oldest of festival offerings and as popular now as they ever were. Through sweet pastry cases and gooey chocolate cakes, the section moves on to cocktail snacks and hors d'œuvres, and then, in a sweeter vein, to chocolates and candies for children to make; from chocolate truffles and other sweetmeats to delectable sugared fruits, flowers and petals to serve with pride at the end of a perfect meal.

FRUIT CAKES WITH A DIFFERENCE

IF YOU wish to serve a cake that is even richer, more moist and even more self-indulgent than the traditional Christmas cake, try this Creole Christmas Cake recipe. However, be prepared for the shock to the budget occasioned by the inclusion of three kinds of spirit and one fortified wine!

The cake is made in celebration of Christmas and other festivals in the West Indies where it has become *the* cake for high-days and holidays among the sugar planters.

By contrast, and in a lighter vein, there is a recipe for Dundee Cake, a preferred option for those who do not care for or cannot take the richer delights of the season.

LEFT: *Oozing with the fruits of a week-long marinade, the Creole Cake is a tempting teatime treat.*

CREOLE CHRISTMAS CAKE

This is a plan-ahead cake which is made in two stages. First the fruit and spices are soaked in the alcohol for 1 week, and the remaining ingredients are added just before baking. It is best made at least 4 weeks before Christmas.

INGREDIENTS

450g/1lb/2²/₃ cups seedless raisins
225g/8oz/1¹/₃ cups currants
100g/4oz/²/₃ cup sultanas (golden raisins)
100g/4oz/²/₃ cup pitted no-soak prunes, chopped
100g/4oz/³/₄ cup candied orange peel, chopped
100g/4oz/²/₃ cup chopped walnuts
4tbsp soft dark brown sugar
1tsp vanilla extract
1tsp ground cinnamon
¹/₄tsp grated nutmeg
¹/₄tsp ground cloves
1tsp salt
4tbsp dark rum
4tbsp brandy
4tbsp whisky
4tbsp port

FOR THE SECOND STAGE

225g/8oz/2 cups plain (all-purpose) flour
1tsp baking powder
225g/8oz/1 cup demerara (light brown) sugar
225g/8oz/1 cup unsalted butter, at room temperature, plus extra for greasing
4 eggs, beaten

FOR THE TOPPING

225g/8oz/1 cup apricot jam, sieved
2tbsp water
pecan halves, to decorate
crystallized tangerine or kumquat slices, to decorate

1 Put all the first list of ingredients into a large, heavy pan, stir and mix well and heat very gently to simmering point. On no account allow the mixture to boil, or the flavour of the alcohol will be lost. Simmer, still very gently, for 15 minutes.

2 Remove the pan from the heat and set aside to cool. Pour the mixture into a lidded jar and leave in the refrigerator for 7 days, stirring at least once every day.

3 To cook the cake, line a 22.5-cm/9-in round cake tin (pan) with a double thickness of non-stick baking paper and grease it well. Heat the oven to 140°C/275°F/Gas 1.

4 Place the flour, baking powder, sugar and butter in a large mixing bowl and beat until smooth. Beat in the eggs, a little at a time, until the mixture is smooth and well blended.

5 Gradually fold in the fruit mixture and stir until it is well blended. Lack of care at this stage could result in an uneven distribution of the fruit.

6 Spoon the mixture into the prepared tin and level the surface. Bake in the centre of the oven for 3 hours, then cover with a double thickness of non-stick baking paper or foil and continue baking for 1 hour, or until the cake feels springy when pressed in the centre.

7 Transfer the tin to a wire rack and leave it to cool. When the cake is completely cold, remove it from the tin, peel off the baking papers and wrap it closely in two thicknesses of foil. The cake will keep well for up to 1 year.

8 A day or two before serving, decorate the top of the cake. Heat the sieved apricot jam and water in a small pan and brush half of it over the top of the cake. Arrange the nuts and kumquat slices in rows or rings and brush them with the remaining apricot glaze.

Makes 1 22.5-cm/9-in cake

DUNDEE CAKE

INGREDIENTS
225g/8oz/1 cup unsalted butter, softened
225g/8oz/1 cup caster (superfine) sugar
grated rind of 1 orange
5 eggs
225g/8oz/2 cups plain (all-purpose) flour, sifted
50g/2oz/1⁄3 cup ground almonds
100g/4oz/2⁄3 cup currants
100g/4oz/2⁄3 cup sultanas (golden raisins)
100g/4oz/2⁄3 cup seedless raisins
50g/2oz/1⁄3 cup Candied orange peel, chopped

FOR THE TOPPING
50g/2oz/1⁄3 cup blanched halved almonds

1 Line a 17.5-cm/7-in round cake tin (pan) with a double thickness of non-stick baking paper . Heat the oven to 150°C/300°F/Gas 2.

2 Beat the butter, sugar and orange rind until the mixture is light and fluffy. Beat in the eggs one at a time with 1tbsp of the flour. Gradually fold in the remaining flour with a large metal spoon. Stir in the almonds, currants, sultanas (golden raisins), raisins and chopped peel and stir until they are evenly distributed.

3 Spoon the mixture into the prepared tin (pan), level the top and arrange the almonds in a wheel pattern.

4 Bake in the centre of the oven for 2½–3 hours, until a skewer inserted into the centre of the cake comes out clean.

5 Cool the cake in the tin (pan) on a wire rack. When it is cold, remove it from the tin (pan), remove the baking papers and closely wrap it in a double thickness of foil. Store in an airtight tin. It should keep well for 6 months.

Makes 1 17.5-cm/7-in cake

ABOVE: A lighter alternative to a rich fruit cake, Dundee Cake is traditionally decorated with rings of blanched almonds.

CHRISTMAS PUDDING

THE LUXURIOUS pudding with which Christmas is celebrated today, rich with dried fruits, sugar and spices and usually enlivened with a dash of alcohol, has derived over several centuries from frumenty, a thick porridge that was eaten on Christmas Eve. Over the years a variety of fruits and other ingredients were added to the basic mixture – first prunes, which gave rise to the name 'plum pudding', and then meat and suet, the fat that gives the pudding its richness.

You can serve one large pudding or make it in individual moulds. When making the pudding mixture, it is customary to ask everyone in the family, and anyone who happens to be visiting, to stir the pudding and make a secret wish.

TRADITIONAL CHRISTMAS PUDDING

INGREDIENTS
225g/8oz/2 cups plain (all-purpose) flour
1tsp ground cinnamon
½tsp grated nutmeg
½tsp ground allspice
1tbsp salt
100g/4oz/1 cup fresh breadcrumbs
550g/1¼lb/2¾ cups seedless raisins
350g/12oz/2 cups sultanas (golden raisins)
350g/12oz/2 cups currants
150g/6oz/1 cup candied peel, sugar coating removed, chopped
50g/2oz/⅓ cup blanched almonds, chopped
225g/8oz/2 cups soft dark brown sugar
225g/8oz/1 cup shredded suet or soft margarine
4 eggs
200ml/6fl oz/1 cup milk
100ml/4fl oz/½ cup brandy or substitute more milk
melted butter, for greasing

1 Sift the flour, spices and salt into a large mixing bowl. Stir in the breadcrumbs, dried fruits, peel, almonds and sugar. Add the suet or margarine and stir well until all the ingredients are well mixed. Beat together the eggs, milk and brandy if you use it and stir the mixture into the dry ingredients.

2 If you intend to cook the pudding in moulds or pudding basins, brush them lightly with melted butter. Cut circles of non-stick baking paper large enough to cover the top of each mould, allowing for a pleat from side to side which will unfold as the mixture expands. Cut pieces of cloth to similar sizes; unbleached calico or muslin (cheesecloth) is traditional, but you can also use foil. Brush the baking paper with butter.

OPPOSITE: Pottery moulds were often used in Victorian times to give variety to the shape of the pudding. Silver coins and charms were sometimes pressed into the mixture and cooked with the pudding as lucky tokens.

3 Spoon the mixture into the moulds to come level with the rims. Cover with the greased and pleated non-stick baking paper and then with a cloth or foil and tie securely with string.

4 To make a round pudding without using a mould, first brush a piece of non-stick baking paper with butter. Place this as a lining on clean, unbleached calico (cheesecloth). Shape the mixture into a round between your hands and bring the paper and the cloth over it. Tie two of the four corners of the cloth into a knot and then, crosswise, tie the other two.

5 Place a trivet of a piece of folded cloth in a large saucepan, add water to come half-way up the mould or the pudding cloth and bring it to the boil. Add the puddings, cover the pan and boil for 5 hours; individual puddings for 2 hours. Top up with more boiling water as needed.

6 Take out the puddings and allow them to cool. Replace the non-stick baking paper and cloths with fresh ones. Store in a cool, dry, airy place. The puddings should keep well for 1 year.

Makes 5 450g/1lb puddings

SERVING CHRISTMAS PUDDINGS

To reheat the puddings on a conventional cooker, boil for a further 3 hours; individual ones for 1 hour. You can do this in a slow cooker (electric crock pot) to relieve pressure on hob (stove top) space.

You can save a considerable amount of time by cooking Christmas puddings in a microwave. Cover the top of a mould with plastic wrap. Place the pudding on the turntable and cook at Medium for 5 minutes. Leave the pudding for 5 minutes, then cook on medium heat for a further 3 minutes. Allow to cool, then cover with a second layer of plastic wrap. Be sure to use microwave-safe moulds and basins, and not metal ones. To reheat the pudding, cook on medium heat for 2 minutes.

To release a pudding from a mould, run a knife around the inside of the mould. Place a warmed plate over the mould, hold it and the mould firmly together and invert to release the pudding. If it does not easily slide out of the mould, shake it up and down.

MINCEMEAT AND MINCE PIES

MINCE PIES are an essential part of the British culinary tradition, enjoyed with great enthusiasm and in great quantity throughout the Christmas holiday, and then rarely, if ever, offered again until the following year.

Originally mincemeat was, as its name implies, made from minced (ground) meat, as a way of preserving the last scraps of meat culled in the autumn so that it would last throughout the winter. The mixture, which also included fresh and dried fruits, spices and sugar, was simmered for several days and then stored in sealed jars in the cellar or in an outhouse. A seventeenth-century writer described the contemporary mince pie, a huge dish called 'Christmas pie',

as 'a most learned mixture of Neats-tongues [ox tongues], chicken, eggs, sugar, raisins, lemon and orange peel, various kinds of Spicery, etc'.

Today's mincemeat no longer contains meat or poultry, except in the form of suet. Those who do not wish to eat animal fats may substitute vegetarian suet, which is a saturated vegetable fat, or use polyunsaturated margarine.

The mixture may be used to fill tray bakes (bars) such as Mincemeat Slice and open lattice flans (pies); spooned into partly baked individual tart shells topped with fancy cut-out pastry shapes, or, when baked and cooled, drizzled with glacé icing.

LEFT : Mincemeat should be made at least 4 weeks before Christmas and left in a cool, dry, dark place to mature.

TRADITIONAL MINCEMEAT

INGREDIENTS
225g/8oz/1 1/3 cups currants
225g/8oz/1 1/3 cups sultanas (golden raisins)
450g/1lb/2 2/3 cups seedless raisins
450g/1lb cooking apples, peeled, cored and chopped
225g/8oz/1 1/2 cups Candied citrus peel, chopped
100g/4oz/2/3 cup blanched almonds, chopped
225g/8oz/1 cup shredded suet, or vegetarian suet
225g/8oz/1 cup soft dark brown sugar
1tsp ground cinnamon
1tsp ground allspice
1tsp ground ginger
1/2tsp grated nutmeg
grated rind and juice of 2 oranges
grated rind and juice of 2 lemons
about 150ml/1/4pt/2/3 cup brandy or port

1 Place all the ingredients except the brandy or port in a large mixing bowl. Stir well, cover the bowl with a cloth and set aside in a cool place overnight.

2 The following day, stir in enough brandy or port to make a mixture moist enough to drop from a spoon.

3 Spoon the mixture into sterilized jars and cover and store in a cool, dry place.

ABOVE RIGHT: Three ways of decorating mince pies: dusted with icing (confectioners') sugar, decorated with holly-leaf shape cut-outs and, open top, drizzled with glacé icing.

DOUBLE-CRUST MINCE PIES

INGREDIENTS

*Shortcrust pastry made with 350g/
12oz/3 cups flour
flour for dusting
450g/1lb/2 cups mincemeat
butter, for greasing
milk, for brushing
icing (confectioners') sugar or caster
(superfine) sugar, for dusting*

1   Heat the oven to 200°C/
400°F/Gas 6. Roll out the
pastry as thinly as possible on a
lightly floured board. Using a
7.5-cm/3-in plain round cutter,
cut out 24 circles. With a 5-cm/
2-in plain round cutter, cut out
another 24 circles.

2   Grease 24 patty tins
(muffin pans), dust them
with flour and line them with the
larger circles. Fill each one with
mincemeat, then brush the edges
with milk. Press the smaller
rounds on top and seal the edges.
Brush the tops with milk.

3   Bake for 25–30 minutes
until the pastry is light
golden brown. Cool in the tins
(pans), then transfer the pies to a
wire rack to become cold. Store
them in an airtight tin. Just
before serving, dust the tops with
sugar. Serve warm.

Makes 24 pies

MINCEMEAT LATTICE FLAN

Mincemeat Lattice Flan is
traditionally served warm
with brandy butter or rum
butter spooned on top.

1   Line a 20-cm/8-in flan case
with shortcrust pastry made
with 225g/8oz/2 cups flour.

2   Spoon in 225g/8oz/1 cup
mincemeat and cut the
remaining pastry in strips 6mm/
¼in wide.

3   Dampen the edges of the
flan case and arrange the
strips to criss-cross each other to
form a lattice effect. Brush the
strips with milk before baking.
Serve warm.

MINCEMEAT SLICE

1   Make Mincemeat Slice in a
similar way to Double-
crust Mince Pies. Use just over
half the rolled pastry to line the
base and sides of a greased tin or
loaf pan 25 × 17.5 cm/10
× 7 in.

2   Brush the side edges with
milk, spoon on the
mincemeat and level the surface
with a knife.

3   Cover with the remaining
pastry, press it firmly on
the edges and trim it neatly all
round. Brush the top with milk
before baking.

4   Just before serving, dust the
top with icing
(confectioners') sugar or caster
(superfine) sugar. Serve warm.

GINGERBREAD

IN ALL its forms, gingerbread has been part of the Christmas tradition for generations. Nowhere was ginger more prized than in Germany, and it is from that country that many present-day traditions originate. By the seventeenth century, every northern-European country had its regional variations of the spiced bread. There were Flemish, Dutch and Swiss specialities, all recognizably closely related to the German ones, and in England gingerbread sold at country fairs, as 'fairings', was often gilded with edible gold leaf. In the United States, gingerbread has been popular since the early colonial days, when Salem, Massachusetts, was an important spice trading centre.

DARK GINGERBREAD

An alternative and somewhat richer recipe than is traditional, this mixture can be used to shape the gingerbread tree ornaments and biscuits (cookies) shown throughout this book; the hearts that comprise the table-centre ring on these pages; and family traditions of your own.

INGREDIENTS

350g/12oz/3 cups plain (all-purpose) flour, plus extra for dusting
2tsp ground ginger
1tsp ground allspice
1tsp ground cinnamon
pinch of salt
1/2tsp bicarbonate of soda (baking soda)
175g/6oz/3/4 cup unsalted butter, at room temperature, plus extra for greasing
4tbsp soft light or dark brown sugar
8tbsp molasses
6tbsp milk

TO DECORATE

100g/4oz/1 cup icing (confectioners') sugar
4–5tsp water or lemon juice
colouring, optional

ABOVE: These gingerbread shapes have been 'gilded' with gold-coloured powder. This is available in both edible and inedible forms.

LEFT: An old Dutch gingerbread mould, shown with fresh, dry and ground ginger, is an example of the intricate shapes that were baked in the eighteenth century.

1 Sift the flour, ginger, allspice, cinnamon, salt and bicarbonate of soda (baking soda) into a bowl.

2 Beat the butter until it is soft, then beat in the sugar and molasses until the mixture is light and fluffy. Gradually stir in the flour and milk alternately, continuing to stir until it is well blended.

3 Knead the dough on a lightly floured board until it is smooth. Place it in a polythene bag and chill in the refrigerator for at least 2 hours or overnight.

4 Heat the oven to 190°C/ 375°F/Gas 5. Lightly grease 2 baking sheets. Roll out the dough to a thickness of 4mm/ 1/8in and cut it to the required shapes. Gather up the trimmings, re-roll the dough and cut out more shapes. If the shapes are to be hung on the tree, push a hole near the top of each one with a skewer.

5 Transfer the shapes to the baking sheets and bake for 10–12 minutes, until the gingerbread is golden brown and beginning to darken at the edges. Leave it to cool slightly on the baking sheets, then transfer to a wire rack to cool.

6 To decorate the shapes, sift the icing (confectioners') sugar into a bowl, mix it to a stiff paste with the water or lemon juice and add colouring of your choice. Spoon the glacé icing into a piping bag and pipe lines, stars, names and other designs.

MOIST GINGERBREAD CAKE

INGREDIENTS

225g/8oz/2 cups plain (all-purpose) flour

2tsp ground ginger

1tsp ground cinnamon

1/4tsp grated nutmeg

pinch of salt

50g/2oz/1/3 cup pitted dates, chopped

50g/2oz/1/3 cup crystallized (candied) ginger, chopped

125g/5oz/1/2 cup black treacle (molasses)

50g/2oz/1/4 cup butter

1 egg

75g/3oz/1/2 cup dark brown sugar

4tbsp milk

1/2tsp bicarbonate of soda (baking soda)

1 Heat the oven to 180°C/350°F/Gas 4. Sift the flour, ginger, cinnamon, nutmeg and salt and stir in the chopped dates and ginger.

2 Melt the treacle (molasses) and butter in a small pan. Beat the egg and beat in the sugar. Add the two mixtures alternately to the dry ingredients, beating all the time. Stir the bicarbonate of soda (baking soda) into the milk, and stir into the mixture.

3 Pour the mixture into a 20cm-/8in square baking tin (pan) lined with non-stick baking paper. Level the top and bake for 45–50 minutes.

BELOW: Use the illustration as a guide for the stencil.

4 Stand the tin on a wire rack to cool. Remove the cake from the tin (pan), strip off the baking paper and wrap the cake in foil. Store it in an airtight tin. It will keep fresh for up to 8 weeks.

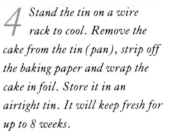

5 Use stiff card (posterboard) for the stencil, so that it can be lifted off without bending. Sift the icing (confectioners') sugar evenly over the top of the cake.

6 Lift off the stencil carefully, holding it at each side.

GINGERBREAD HEART RING

This table centre-piece is inspired by traditional Polish Christmas decorations. You could make one with other cut-out shapes such as gingerbread men and women, teddy bears or stars.

EQUIPMENT

* 7 heart-shaped gingerbread biscuits, baked and decorated
* stiff cardboard ring, outer diameter 25cm/10in, inner measurement 15cm/6in
* glacé icing made with 100g/ 4oz/1 cup sifted icing (confectioners') sugar and, if you wish, coloured red
* 5cm/2in-wide ribbon
* Victorian-style paper scraps (optional)

1 Cover the cardboard ring with glacé icing and quickly – before it sets – press on the heart-shaped gingerbread to cover it.

RIGHT: Victorian scraps or other paper decorations can be fixed to the centre of each biscuit with a dab of glacé icing.

2 Tie the ribbon into a bow, trim the ends and fix it to the ring with a generous dab of glacé icing to ensure it stays securely in place throughout the season. To preserve the ring as a decoration throughout the Christmas holidays, it may be as well to make extra heart-shaped biscuits (cookies) for young gingerbread enthusiasts to eat!

HORS D'OEUVRES AND CANAPÉS

PASTRY PLAYS a leading role at Christmastime, whether for delicious appetizers before an extended meal, or a tray of hors d'œuvres to serve at a drinks party. These recipes will help you to plan and prepare your menus with ease.

CHEESE STRAWS

Make cheese straws in a similar way to Festive Nibbles. Replace the seed topping with 25g/1oz/½ cup grated cheese.

1 *Cut the cheese pastry into fingers about 10cm/4in long and 6mm/¼in wide.*

2 *With the trimmings, cut rounds using 2 pastry cutters of different sizes, a 6cm/2½in one to cut out the circle and a 5cm/2in diameter one to stamp out the centre.*

3 *To serve the Cheese Straws push 6 or 8 straws through each ring.*

Makes about 50 straws and 8 rings

FESTIVE NIBBLES

The more the merrier — stars, crescent moons, triangles, squares, hearts, fingers and rounds. Shape these spicy cheese snacks in any way you wish, serve them with drinks from ice-cold cocktails to hot and spicy mulls.

INGREDIENTS

100g/4oz/1 cup plain (all-purpose) flour, plus extra for dusting
1tsp mustard powder
salt
100g/4oz/½ cup butter, plus extra for greasing
75g/3oz Cheddar cheese, grated
pinch of cayenne
2tbsp water
1 egg, beaten
poppy seeds, sunflower seeds or sesame seeds, to decorate

1 *Heat the oven to 200°C/400°F/Gas 6. Sift the flour, mustard powder and salt into a bowl and rub in the butter until the mixture resembles fine breadcrumbs. Stir in the cheese and cayenne and sprinkle on the water. Add half the beaten egg, mix to a firm dough and knead lightly until smooth.*

2 *Roll out the dough onto a lightly floured board and cut out a variety of shapes. Re-roll the trimmings and cut more shapes.*

3 *Place the shapes on a greased baking sheet and brush the tops with the remaining egg. Sprinkle on the seeds to decorate.*

LEFT: Festive fare includes Buttermilk Scones and Palmiers.

OPPOSITE: Cheese Straws and Festive Nibbles make an appetizing display.

YOUNG COOKS

CHILDREN OF all ages love to help in the kitchen – rolling out pastry, licking out the cake bowl, and sometimes even helping to wash the dishes. But most of all, young cooks like to have a project of their own, a recipe they can follow from start to finish and serve or give away to friends with pride.

FRUIT AND NUT CLUSTERS

INGREDIENTS

225g/8oz white chocolate, broken into pieces
50g/2oz/1/3 cup sunflower seeds
50g/2oz/1/3 cup almond slivers
50g/2oz/1/3 cup sesame seeds
50g/2oz/1/3 cup seedless raisins
1 tsp ground cinnamon

EQUIPMENT

* weighing scales
* mixing bowl
* spoon
* wooden spoon
* heatproof bowl
* pan of simmering water
* 2 teaspoons
* about 24 paper sweet cases (candy cups)

BELOW: The chocolate mounds in paper cases are displayed on a bright fan, an attractive way to present them at a youngsters' party.

ABOVE: Nuts and seeds, raisins and white chocolate have all the makings of delicious Fruit and Nut Clusters.

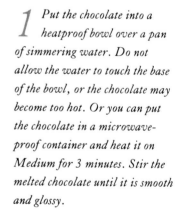

1 *Put the chocolate into a heatproof bowl over a pan of simmering water. Do not allow the water to touch the base of the bowl, or the chocolate may become too hot. Or you can put the chocolate in a microwave-proof container and heat it on Medium for 3 minutes. Stir the melted chocolate until it is smooth and glossy.*

2 *Mix all the other ingredients together, pour on the chocolate and mix well.*

3 *Using 2 teaspoons, spoon the mixture into paper cases and leave to set. Store in an airtight tin.*

Makes about 24 clusters

CHOCOLATE MAGICS

Children will love to see the magic transformation of these biscuits (cookies) after baking.

INGREDIENTS

250g/9oz plain (semi-sweet) chocolate, broken into pieces
100g/4oz/½ cup unsalted butter, cut into pieces
75g/3oz/⅓ cup caster (superfine) sugar
3 eggs
1tsp vanilla extract
150g/6oz/1½ cups plain (all-purpose) flour
½tsp baking powder
3tbsp unsweetened cocoa powder
large pinch of salt
about 75g/3oz/1 cup icing (confectioners') sugar, for coating

EQUIPMENT

* weighing scales
* medium saucepan
* knife
* wooden spoon
* saucer
* medium-sized bowl
* tablespoon
* sieve
* plastic wrap
* 2 baking sheets
* non-stick baking paper
* small bowl
* 2 teaspoons
* 2 wire cooling racks
* spatula

1 Put the chocolate and butter into the saucepan and melt it over a low heat, stirring it with the wooden spoon several times. Remove the pan from the heat and stir in the sugar. Break each egg into a saucer and add them one at a time to the chocolate mixture. Stir in the vanilla extract.

2 Sift the flour, baking powder, cocoa and salt into the bowl. Gradually add the melted chocolate mixture, stirring all the time. When the mixture is smooth and well blended, cover the bowl with plastic wrap and place it in the refrigerator for at least 2 hours.

3 To cook the biscuits (cookies), heat the oven to 170°C/325°F/Gas 3. Cover the baking sheet with a piece of non-stick baking paper.

4 Sift the icing (confectioners') sugar into the small bowl. Using a teaspoon, scoop out the chocolate mixture and push it off the spoon and into your hand with the other teaspoon. Roll the mixture between your palms to make a ball – your hands have to be very clean to do this – and drop it into the bowl of icing (confectioners') sugar. Roll it until it is well covered in sugar then place it on the baking sheet. Continue until all the mixture is used up, placing the chocolate rounds at least 7.5cm/3in apart.

5 Bake the biscuits (cookies) for 10–12 minutes, until they feel soft and springy when touched. Place the baking sheets on the wire cooling racks for a few minutes. Lift off the biscuits (cookies) with a spatula and arrange them on the racks. When they are cold, store them in an airtight tin.

Makes about 24 biscuits (cookies)

BELOW: *The refrigerated Chocolate Magic paste is shaped into small balls and dipped in sifted icing (confectioners') sugar. At this stage they look like chocolate truffles.*

BOTTOM: *Who would guess that the chocolate rounds would have a crazy-paving, sugar topping like this? No wonder they are called Chocolate Magics!*

MAKING CANDIES

CANDIES AND sweets of all kinds have a multiplicity of roles at Christmastime. Making them at home in a cosy kitchen is fun and children love to help. They may be able to spoon out the honey, shell the nuts, roll truffles in coloured hundreds and thousands (coloured sprinkles), or pack the finished items in a box as a special present – home-made candies and chocolate are among the most welcome of gifts. A glance at the price of the candies in specialist shops leaves no doubt that these are firmly in the luxury class. Packed in a different way, wrapped in check gingham fabric and tied with pretty ribbons, sliced candy makes delightful Christmas tree decorations which guests will just love to take home.

HONEY AND NUT CLUSTER

This is a popular candy in Italy, where it is known as 'Torrone'. To serve, cut it in squares or fingers and keep it in the refrigerator. It is delightfully sticky!

INGREDIENTS
100g/4oz/²/3 cup blanched almonds
100g/4oz/1 cup shelled hazelnuts (filberts)
whites of 2 eggs
100g/4oz/¹/2 cup clear honey
100g/4oz/¹/2 cup caster (superfine) sugar

1   *Line a 20-cm/8-in square tin (pan) with non-stick baking paper.*

2   *Spread the almonds and hazelnuts (filberts) on separate baking sheets and toast them in the oven at the lowest temperature for about 30 minutes. Tip onto a cloth and rub off the skins. Roughly chop both types of nut.*

3   *Whisk the egg whites until they are stiff and stir in the chopped nuts.*

4   *Put the honey and sugar into a small, heavy pan and bring to the boil. Stir in the nut mixture and continue cooking over a moderate heaat for 10 minutes.*

5   *Turn the mixture into the prepared tin (pan) and level the top. Cover with another piece of non-stick paper, put weights (such as food cans) on top and leave in the refrigerator for at least 2 days.*

6   *To present the Torrone as a tree decoration, wrap slices in non-stick baking paper and then in gift-wrap or cotton fabric, or in foil.*

LEFT: Slices of the Honey and Nut Cluster, wrapped in non-stick baking paper and pink check gingham, make pretty take- home gifts.

CHOCOLATE TRUFFLES

These rich and irresistible sweet meats are always popular. Even after the most sumptuous of meals, you will not find a guest who will refuse one. You can coat the truffle mixture in a variety of ways – with melted milk or white chocolate; rolled in unsweetened cocoa powder; or covered in hundreds and thousands (coloured sprinkles).

INGREDIENTS
150ml/¼pt/⅔ cup double (heavy) cream
250g/9oz bitter or plain (semi-sweet) chocolate, broken into pieces
2tbsp brandy or rum
about 3tbsp cocoa powder, for dusting

1 Pour the cream into a heavy pan and bring to the boil. Remove from the heat and add the chocolate. Stir until melted and well blended. Stir in the brandy or rum and strain into a bowl. Set aside to cool, then chill for at least 1 hour.

2 Using a melon baller with a 2-cm/¾-in scoop, or 2 small teaspoons, form the mixture into balls and place them on a baking sheet lined with non-stick baking paper. Chill for 1 hour.

3 Sift about 3tbsp cocoa into a small bowl. Roll the truffles in the cocoa to coat them on all sides – turning them over and over with a wooden cocktail stick or toothpick keeps the coating intact. Place them in small paper cases and store them in a box in the refrigerator. Remove them about 30 minutes before serving.

RIGHT: Fancy truffles are ready to be placed in paper cases and stored in the refrigerator.

BELOW: Cocoa-coated truffles piled into an engraved glass dish are shown to advantage with a single gilded leaf. It is not customary to make these truffles perfectly round.

SUGARED FLOWERS AND FRUITS

SPARKLING UNDER a light dusting of caster (superfine) sugar like summer fruits and flowers unseasonally tinged with frost or snow, sugared sweetmeats are a delicacy especially suited to the magic of Christmas. You can prepare them several days in advance of the festivities and, once they are thoroughly dry, store them in an airtight tin.

Make your selection of flowers and fruits, petals and leaves as appetizing and visually appealing as you can. Christmas is a time for giving way to culinary temptation and visual flights of fancy.

It may be a case of gathering the last of the season's roses or using petals from a rose in a bouquet. Enjoy the flowers in an arrangement for a day or two and then, while they are still in their prime, and certainly before they begin to discolour, pluck off the petals for sugaring.

Not all flowers are edible, though many are. Check with the list on this page before gathering others for your sugar collection. Marigolds, nasturtiums and pansies were all favourites in Victorian times, and offer an attractive variety of colour and shapes.

Sugared fruits add substantially to a sweetmeat selection. You can process small fruits such as cherries, cranberries, strawberries and raspberries whole. Larger ones such as oranges and tangerines should be peeled and segmented, figs halved or quartered, according to their size, and plums and apricots halved and pitted.

Sugared leaves are a pretty contrast to both fruit and flowers. The sugared leaves can be used with fruit and flowers to add a notion of realism, or composed into dainty herbal sprays, a neat decoration for a dessert or cheesecake.

ABOVE: After dipping in egg white, a rose petal is lightly dusted with caster (superfine) sugar to cover the whole surface.

LEFT: Sugared rose petals and cranberries are arranged in the shape of a flower with variegated mint leaves. This decoration can be used on a cake or dessert.

GUIDE TO EDIBLE FLOWERS

Crystallizing (candying) flowers and petals is such a delightful task that it is easy to get carried away and preserve every flower in sight. It is important to remember that not all flowers or plants are edible, and some may be harmful. If you are in doubt about the safety or suitability of any plant, consult a reliable source, or confine your decorative activities to those on the list below.

almond blossom (*Prunus dulcis*)
apple blossom (*Malus sylvestris*)
borage (*Borago officianalis*)
carnation (*Dianthus caryophyllus*)
clover (*Trifolium sp.*)
cowslip (*Primula veris*)
daisy (*Bellis perennis*)
dandelion (*Taraxacum officinale*)
elderflower (*Sambucus nigra*)
forget-me-not (*Myosotis alpestris*)
freesia (*Freesia x kewenis*)
honeysuckle (*Lonicera periclymenum*)
hydrangea (*Hydrangea macrophylla*)
jasmine (*Jasminium officinale*)
lavender (*Lavandula vera*)
magnolia (*Magnolia grandiflora*)
may blossom (*Crataegus monogyna*)
mimosa (*Acacia dealbata*)
nasturtium (*Tropaeolum majus*)
orange blossom (*Citrus sinensis*)
pansy (*Viola tricolor*)
primrose (*Primula vulgaris*)
rose (*Rosa gallica*)
scented-leaf geranium (*Pelargonium graveolens*)
sweet william (*Dianthus barabatus*)
violet (*Viola odorata*)
yarrow (*Achillea millefolium*)

ABOVE RIGHT: An orange segment held on a skewer is dipped into a bowl of lightly beaten egg white.

RIGHT: Flowers, petals and fruits dipped in egg white and dusted with sugar are left to dry on a wire rack covered with non-stick baking paper.

BREADS, SCONES AND TEABREADS

WITH so many rich, traditional foods featured on the Christmas menus, it can be a welcome change to be offered a slice of delicious home-made bread with butter or cheese, or a light-as-a-feather scone with a choice of preserves. And with the coming and going of expected and unexpected guests, it is a good idea to have a stand-by recipe for a bread suitable for all occasions.

These three recipes offer just such versatility. The Irish Soda Bread takes only moments to make and as it uses soda as the raising agent, is not left to rise between making and baking.

The Cheese Scone recipe makes a welcome change from the rich foods of the season, and may be served at a light brunch or lunch. Vary the flavour with herbs or seeds.

Lastly Stollen, a yeast bread speckled with fruit and sprinkled with icing (confectioners') sugar, is an Austrian speciality which may be eaten plain – it is slightly sweet – or with butter or preserves, and is delicious toasted.

ABOVE AND BELOW: Soda Bread with its soft, crumbly texture is a good choice for an informal snack, and contrasts well with other breads for a cheese and wine party.

IRISH SODA BREAD

INGREDIENTS
450g/1lb/4 cups plain (all-purpose) flour
2tsp bicarbonate of soda (baking soda)
1tsp salt
300ml/1/2pt/1 1/4 cups milk

1   Heat the oven to 220°C/ 425°F/Gas 7. Sift the flour, soda and salt into a bowl. Pour on the milk and mix to a soft dough.

2   Turn the dough onto a lightly floured board and knead it lightly until smooth. Shape it into a round and stand it on a greased and floured baking sheet. Cut a cross in the top and brush with milk.

3   Bake in the oven for 35–40 minutes, until the loaf is well risen and golden brown. Cool on a wire rack.

Makes 1 loaf

CHEESE SCONES

INGREDIENTS

225g/8oz/2 cups plain (all-purpose) flour
1tsp cream of tartar
1tsp bicarbonate of soda (baking soda)
1tsp dry mustard powder
pinch salt and pepper
1–2tsp chopped fresh herbs (optional)
50g/2oz/1/2 cup butter
75g/3oz/1/3 cup grated cheese
150ml/1/4pt/2/3 cup milk or buttermilk

1 Sift the flour, cream of tartar, soda, mustard and salt and pepper into a bowl. Add the fresh herbs, if using. Rub in the fat until the mixture is like dry breadcrumbs, and gradually stir in enough milk to make a light, springy dough. Stir in the grated cheese.

2 Turn the dough onto a lightly floured board and knead until smooth. Roll it to a thickness of 2.5cm/1in. Cut into rounds with a 5-cm/2-in cutter (or a 4-cm/11/2-in cutter for cocktail savouries). Place the scones on a floured baking sheet and brush the tops with milk. Bake in the oven for 7–10 minutes, until the scones are well risen and golden brown.

Makes about 16 scones

STOLLEN

INGREDIENTS

150ml/1/4pt/2/3 cup lukewarm milk
40g/11/2oz/3tbsp caster (superfine) sugar
2tsp dried yeast
350g/12oz/5 cups plain (all-purpose) flour, plus extra for dusting
1/4tsp salt
100g/4oz/1/2 cup butter, softened
1 egg, beaten
50g/2oz/1/3 cup seedless raisins
25g/1oz/1/6 cup sultanas (golden raisins)
40g/11/2oz/1/3 cup candied orange peel, chopped
25g/1oz/1/2 cup blanched almonds, chopped
1tbsp rum
40g/11/2oz/3tbsp butter, melted
about 50g/2oz/1/2 cup icing (confectioners') sugar

1 Mix together the warm milk, sugar and yeast and leave it in a warm place until it is frothy.

2 Sift together the flour and salt, make a well in the centre, pour on the yeast mixture. Add the softened butter and egg and mix to form a soft dough. Mix in the raisins, sultanas (golden raisins), peel and almonds and sprinkle on the rum. Knead the dough on a lightly floured board until it is pliable.

3 Place the dough in a greased bowl, cover it with non-stick baking paper and set it aside in a warm place for about 2 hours, until it has doubled in size.

4 Turn the dough out onto a floured board and knead it lightly until it is smooth and elastic again. Shape the dough to a rectangle about 25 × 20cm/10 × 8in. Fold the dough over along one of the long sides and press the 2 layers together. Cover the loaf and leave it to stand for 20 minutes.

ABOVE: Stollen, a fruity yeast bread traditionally served in Austria at Christmastime, may be served at breakfast, coffee or teatime.

5 Heat the oven to 200°C/400°F/Gas 6. Bake the loaf in the oven for 25–30 minutes, until it is well risen. Allow it to cool slightly on the baking sheet, then brush it with melted butter. Sift the sugar over the top and transfer the loaf to a wire rack to cool.

Makes 1 loaf

FESTIVE FOOD AND DRINKS

Welcome and pamper your Christmas guests with drinks that sparkle and bubble, with colourful cocktails tingling with ice, and with mulls and punches heady with the aroma of fruit and spices, spirits and wine.

Throughout the holidays there may be times when only chilled Champagne or classic Champagne cocktails will match the mood of the moment. At other times it may be more appropriate to serve a heart-warming mull that makes it easy for guests to be of good cheer.

Whatever the occasion, rise to it with a selection of snacks and nibbles, most of which you can have in store before you even issue any invitations.

WELCOME, CHRISTMAS

CHAMPAGNE AND other sparkling wine cocktails have just what it takes to welcome Christmas guests and callers. Buck's fizz is a sparky accompaniment to a late breakfast or a leisurely brunch when the main meal is to be served in the evening, and bubbly cocktails have the sparkle to set the scene as the family – or at least the adult members of it – get into the swing of Christmas mid-morning.

Purists avow that nothing but the best is good enough to comprise Christmas Day cocktails – and Champagne certainly has a quality and taste that no other sparkling wine can quite match. However, when the cocktails are to be flavoured – and delightfully coloured, too – with Cassis, grenadine syrup or peach syrup – as the trio of drinks here – then who is to quibble if you use a good-quality sparkling white wine? The French Veuve du Vernay, a German sparkling hock, the New Zealand Lindauer

FESTIVE FOOD AND DRINKS

Brut or the Californian Domaine Chandon are all suitable candidates.

Experiment with fruit juices and flavourings such as cranberry juice, peach and apricot nectar and elderflower cordial. Add a dash of brandy, white rum or vodka to give the cocktail an extra kick and a scattering of fruit to give it style. Twists and slices of lemon, lime and orange decorating the rim of each glass create definite eye appeal, and strawberries and raspberries, grapes, sliced mangoes, kiwi fruits (Chinese gooseberries) and passion fruits add immeasurably to the appeal of 'wine cups' from a bowl.

Remember to chill white or rosé wines well in advance of serving and, for the extra tingle factor, chill the glasses too. Then dip the moist rims in caster (superfine) sugar to give them a seasonally frosty look. Have all the other ingredients ready, the flavourings, fruit and mixers such as lemonade and mineral water, and add the bubbly last of all.

POMEGRANATE PINKER

INGREDIENTS
30ml/1fl oz/2tbsp grenadine syrup
15ml/¹/2fl oz/1tbsp brandy
(optional)
250ml/8fl oz/1 cup Champagne or other sparkling white wine, chilled
twist of thinly pared lemon peel

Put the grenadine syrup into a chilled glass, mix in the brandy if you use it and pour on the wine. Mix the drink with a swizzle stick or slender spoon and add the lemon peel. Serve at once.

Makes 1 glass

A PEACH OF A DRINK

INGREDIENTS
30ml/1fl oz/2tbsp peach syrup
15ml/¹/2fl oz/1 tbsp vodka
(optional)
250ml/8fl oz/1 cup Champagne or other sparkling white wine, chilled
2 thin slices of lime

Put the peach syrup into a chilled glass, mix in the vodka if you use it and pour on the wine. Mix the drink with a swizzle stick or slender spoon. Cut the lime slices from the outside to the centre and balance them on the rim of the glass. Serve at once.

Makes 1 glass

SPARKLING KIR

INGREDIENTS
330ml/1fl oz/2 tbsp Cassis
250ml/8fl oz/1 cup Champagne or other sparkling white wine, chilled
1 slice of orange, halved

Put the Cassis into a chilled glass, top it up with the wine and mix well. Garnish with an orange slice. Serve at once.

Makes 1 glass

ABOVE: *Three Champagne cocktails match the mood of the moment. Pomegranate Pinker decorated with a twist of lemon peel, a Peach of a Drink, with slices of lime, and Sparkling Kir with orange slices.*

COCKTAIL TIME

Turn back the clock sometime over Christmas and serve thirties-style cocktails. Put cracked ice into a cocktail shaker or a glass, add a dash of this, a measure of that and a spark of ingenuity and serve the concoction with style. This may mean a twist of orange or lemon peel for its colour, its oil and its aroma, or a sprig of mint, a maraschino cherry, a cocktail onion or an olive speared on a pretty cocktail umbrella.

Serve cocktails in glasses that have been polished until they shine and, whenever possible, chilled to the same low temperature as the drink itself. Where refrigerator space is at a premium and a tray of glasses placed on the lowest shelf is not an option, if the weather is cold, the outside temperature may come to the rescue. Cover the glasses with a cloth and leave them in the garage, car port or on the balcony while you make the final preparations. The cocktails will be all the more refreshing if the glasses are chilled.

GRENADINE SLING

INGREDIENTS
3 dashes of Angostura bitters
juice of ½ lime
15ml/½fl oz/1 tbsp grenadine
syrup
45ml/1½fl oz/3 tbsp gin
cracked ice
soda water
twist of orange peel

Put the bitters, lime juice, grenadine and gin into a 300-ml/ ½-pt/1¼-cup glass and add cracked ice. Fill with soda water and stir lightly. Decorate with orange peel.

Makes 1 glass

APRICOT SOUR

INGREDIENTS
8 dashes Angostura bitters
200ml/6fl oz/¾ cup apricot
brandy
2tsp caster (superfine) sugar
30ml/2fl oz/¼ cup lemon juice
cracked ice
4 maraschino cherries, to decorate

Put all the ingredients except the cherries into a cocktail shaker or screw-top jar and shake vigorously. Strain into 4 chilled glasses and decorate each with a cocktail cherry.

Makes 4 glasses

HORSE'S NECK

INGREDIENTS
1 lemon
8 ice cubes
200ml/8fl oz/1 cup gin
600ml/1pt/2½ cups ginger ale,
chilled

Thinly pare the lemon so that the rind comes off in one long strip, then cut it into 4 thin, curling strips.

Put 2 ice cubes into each of 4 tumblers. Squeeze the juice of the lemon, mix it with the gin and split between the glasses. Top up with ginger ale and add a twist of peel to each.

Makes 4 tumblers

LEFT: Horse's Neck, a gin and ginger ale cocktail, is sharpened with lemon juice and twists of peel.

ICE FANCIES

SCARLETT O'HARA COCKTAIL

This rich-ruby-red-coloured cocktail looks like Christmas all the way. For added style serve it in 'cranberry' glasses.

INGREDIENTS
350ml/12fl oz/1½ cups Southern Comfort
200ml/6fl oz/¾ cup cranberry juice
juice of 1 lime
cracked ice
maraschino cherries, to serve

Put all the ingredients except the cherries into a jug and stir well. Strain into chilled glasses and decorate each one with a cherry.

Makes 8 glasses

You can add fun and flair to cocktails and chilled fruit punches by presenting the ice in stylish ways. For coloured ice cubes, put a few drops of food colouring into a jug of water before pouring it into ice-cube trays, then harmonize the colours of the ice and cocktails, red ice with a pink-hued drink, green ice with a lime-based cocktail, blue-tinged ice with a colourless blend.

Freeze small strawberries, raspberries, blackberries or melon balls in the ice-trays. Place the fruit in each section and then fill it up with water. Ring the changes and freeze a small flower or blossom in a similar way.

You can multiply these notions for a chilled cocktail bowl, so that you can serve a fruit or flower cube with each drink. For an added dimension, freeze ice in biscuit (cookie) cutters covered in foil. Wrap the foil tightly around the base and sides of star, bell, Santa, Christmas tree and other seasonal shapes and place them on a baking sheet.

BELOW: Ice cubes look more festive if you freeze them with fruit and small edible flowers.

BUCK'S FIZZ (MIMOSA)

This delightfully refreshing drink, invented by the barman at the Buck's Club in London in 1921, has achieved star status. In France it is known as 'Champagne-orange' and in Italy and the United States as 'Mimosa'.

BELOW: It's Christmas morning, and present-opening time. A glass of ice-cold Buck's Fizz decorated with a slice of tangy lime adds to the air of excitement.

INGREDIENTS

100ml/4fl oz/1/2 cup fresh orange juice
1 tsp grenadine syrup
200ml/6fl oz/3/4 cup Champagne or other sparkling white wine, chilled

Put the orange juice and grenadine into a chilled glass and top up with wine. Serve at once.

Makes 1 glass

CHAMPAGNE CUP

Layers and layers of pineapple slices over cracked ice, a trio of liqueurs and the fizz of Champagne — what better way to celebrate!

ABOVE: Champagne Cup, with ice-cold layers of fruit and sparkling wine, is a perfect Christmas-morning cocktail.

INGREDIENTS
cracked ice
1 large pineapple, trimmed and thinly sliced
3 large oranges, thinly sliced
1 large cucumber, thinly sliced
45ml/1 1/2fl oz/1/4 cup Maraschino liqueur
45ml/1 1/2fl oz/1/4 cup green Chartreuse
45ml/1 1/2fl oz/1/4 cup brandy
1 bottle dry Champagne or other sparkling white wine, chilled

Place a layer of cracked ice in a chilled punch bowl or serving bowl and arrange layers of pineapple, orange and cucumber slices over it. Repeat the layers of ice and fruit, finishing with fruit. Pour on the liqueurs and brandy and just before serving, pour on the Champagne or wine. Serve in chilled glasses with a little of the fruit in each.

Serves 6—8

ORCHARD FIZZ

Sparkling apple juice has enough of the rising-bubbles factor to qualify as a Christmas morning cocktail for the younger members of the family.

INGREDIENTS
10 sugar cubes
2 lemons, thinly sliced
200ml/6fl oz/3⁄4 cup lime juice
1l/1 3⁄4pt/4 1⁄3 cups sparkling apple juice
250ml/8fl oz/1 cup soda water (club soda)
2 limes, thinly sliced
2 kiwi fruits, peeled and thinly sliced
mint sprigs

Rub the sugar cubes over the lemons to remove the zest and place one in each glass. Squeeze the juice of the lemons and put the juice in a chilled jug with the lime juice, apple juice and soda water. Mix together and float the fruit slices and mint sprigs on top. Serve in chilled glasses.

Makes 10 glasses

BELOW: *Orchard Fizz, a non-alcoholic cocktail, is decorated with thinly sliced limes and kiwi fruit (Chinese gooseberries).*

CRANBERRY FROST

A non-alcoholic cocktail with the colour of holly berries will delight younger and older guests alike. It is the perfect 'one for the road' drink to serve at the end of a gathering.

INGREDIENTS
100g/4oz/1⁄2 cup caster (superfine) sugar
juice of 2 oranges
100ml/4fl oz/1⁄2 cup cranberry juice
1l/1 3⁄4pt/4 1⁄3 cups sparkling mineral water (seltzer)
2–3tbsp fresh cranberries, to decorate
sprigs of mint, to decorate

ABOVE: *The very essence of festive colour, non-alcoholic Cranberry Frost is chilled with fruited ice cubes and decorated with fresh berries.*

Put the sugar, orange juice and water into a small pan and stir over a low heat to dissolve the sugar. Bring to the boil and boil for 3 minutes. Set aside to cool. The syrup can be made in advance and stored in a covered container in the refrigerator. Pour the syrup into a chilled bowl, pour on the cranberry juice and mix well. To serve, pour on the mineral water and decorate with cranberries and mint leaves.

Serves 10

APPETIZERS

BALANCE IS the key word when you are planning the dips and dunks, pastries and nibbles to serve with drinks. Whether the snacks are to be enjoyed as appetizers before a meal or represent the food element of a drinks party, make your selections as varied as possible.

If you use cream cheese as the already-thickened, dairy-rich basis of some of your dips, include at least one such as Chick-pea Dip or Taramasalata that has no cheese, and at least one which is suitable for vegetarians.

Even if pastry-making and shaping is your strong point,

vary your selection of tartlet cases – cut down on preparation time too – by making some from crisply-baked sliced bread and pitta bread rounds, and include some hot finger foods such as Mini Meatballs and Devils on Horseback.

If the snacks are to be served before a meal, allow two or three for each guest. If they are to be served at an informal gathering, allow three or four per guest at lunchtime, four or five in the evening, and be sure to have a supply of nuts, olives and crackers for variety. Provides a stack of small plates or waxed paper plates and napkins to avoid spills.

MINI MEATBALLS

INGREDIENTS
350g/12oz/1½ cups lean minced
(ground) beef
100g/4oz/ bacon, rind removed,
minced
1 tsp dried thyme
grated nutmeg
salt and black pepper
flour, for dusting
vegetable oil, for frying

BARBECUE SAUCE
3 tbsp olive oil
1 large onion, finely chopped
1 clove garlic, finely chopped
2 tsp tomato purée
2 tbsp demerara (light brown)
sugar
2 tbsp red wine vinegar
2 tbsp Worcestershire sauce
150ml/¼pt/⅔ cup chicken stock
or water

1 Mix the beef and bacon together with a wooden spoon until it forms a smooth paste. Stir in the thyme and season with nutmeg, salt and pepper. Cover and chill for at least 1 hour.

2 Dust your hands with flour. Scoop the mixture with a teaspoon and shape it into balls slightly larger than a walnut.

3 Heat some oil in a heavy frying pan (skillet) and fry the meatballs over a moderate heat for about 7 minutes, turning them until they are cooked and evenly brown on all sides. Serve warm, with Barbecue sauce.

4 To make the sauce, heat the oil in a pan and fry the onion and garlic over a moderate heat until the onion is translucent. Stir in the tomato purée and then the remaining ingredients and simmer for 10 minutes. Serve hot.

Makes about 24 meatballs

RIGHT: For eye-catching garnishes press out vegetable shapes using biscuit (cookie) cutters.

CHEESE AND OLIVE BITES

Serve these delicious bite-sized morsels chilled and speared with toothpicks, as an appetizer at a cheese and wine party or a drinks party.

INGREDIENTS
225g/8oz/1 cup soft cream cheese
about 16 stuffed green olives
50g/2oz/⅓ cup chopped walnuts

1 Beat the cheese until it is soft. Take heaped teaspoonfuls of the cheese and shape them around each olive. Roll them between your palms to form neat spherical shapes. Put the chopped walnuts in a saucer and roll the cheese bites in them to cover them evenly. Chill.

2 You can, if you wish, cut the bites in half to show the olives and make the savouries more colourful.

Makes about 16 bites

SCRAMBLED EGGS AND MUSHROOM TARTLETS

INGREDIENTS

Shortcrust pastry made with 225g/
8oz/2 cups plain (all-purpose)
flour
beaten egg, for glazing
25g/1oz/2tbsp butter, plus extra
for greasing
4 eggs
3tbsp single (light) cream
salt and freshly ground black
pepper
100g/4oz/½ cup oyster or button
mushrooms, chopped
black olive 'petals', to garnish

1 Heat the oven to 190°C/
375°F/Gas 5. Make the
pastry and leave it to rest for
15–20 minutes.

2 Roll out the pastry and use
it to line 24 greased tartlet
tins (small baking pans). Brush
the rims with beaten egg and
prick the bases with a fork. Line
each pastry case with a circle of
non-stick baking paper and fill it
with baking beans. Bake the
pastry cases 'blind' for 10
minutes, then remove the beans
and paper and bake for a further
5–7 minutes to dry the pastry.
Remove the tins and stand on a
wire rack.

3 Melt the butter in a small
pan over a moderate heat.
Beat the eggs and cream together
and season with salt and pepper.
Pour the mixture into the pan
and stir until it is beginning to
set. Stir in the chopped
mushrooms and stir until the
mixture is just set but
still creamy.

4 Spoon the filling into the
warm pastry cases and
decorate some with olive 'petals'.
Serve warm.

Makes 24 tartlets

BACON CRISPIES

INGREDIENTS

150g/6oz bacon, rind removed,
finely chopped
150g/6oz/¾ cup butter, softened
175g/6oz/1½ cups plain (all-
purpose) flour
salt and pepper
100g/4oz/½ cup grated Cheddar

1 Fry the bacon in a non-stick
pan over a moderate heat,
stirring frequently, until it is
crisp and dry. Transfer it to a
plate covered with paper towels
and set aside to cool.

ABOVE: *Individual tartlet
cases are filled with scrambled
egg and oyster mushrooms and
garnished with black olive
'petals'.*

2 Heat the oven to 170°C/
325°F/Gas 3. Beat
together the butter, flour, salt
and pepper until smooth. Stir ⅔
of the bacon and the grated cheese
into the mixture and mix well.

3 Place teaspoonfuls of the
mixture well apart on a
greased baking sheet and sprinkle
with the remaining bacon.

4 Bake in the oven for 30
minutes, until lightly
brown. Cool on a wire rack, and
store in an airtight tin.

Makes 28–30 snacks

INFORMAL DRINKS PARTY

WHEN THE music's playing, the candles are flickering and your guests are in the mood to enjoy themselves, a party planned on informal lines or on the spur of the moment can perfectly capture the festive spirit. The drinks can be relatively cheap, with a selection of beer, lager, cider and mineral water and a sparkling cider and fruit cup. And the food can be an appetizing example of self-assembly.

At a 'roll-filling' party, people can help themselves to what they want. You provide a choice of crisp and crunchy, soft and seed-topped white and wholewheat rolls and pitta bread, a platter of cold meats, kebabs and salads for your guests to fill them with – and a warm, relaxed welcome.

SANDWICH FILLINGS

Cold sandwich fillings could include the following:

Meat Slice roast beef, spiced beef, baked ham, roast turkey or salami, garlic sausage and other prepared meats.

Fish This could include smoked salmon, Gravad lax, smoked trout, or smoked mackerel.

Pâté These could be meat- or fish-based, including pheasant and pork pâté or smoked trout pâté.

Eggs Serve scrambled eggs embellished with smoked salmon or oyster mushrooms.

Cheeses Offer a choice of soft and hard cheeses. This might be cream cheese with chopped dates, Mozzarella or Mascarpone cheese. Hard cheeses could include Cheddar, Cheshire or Gloucester. These should be thinly sliced or grated. For ease of serving, they could be mixed with a little cream cheese or lightly whipped double (heavy) cream. Stilton, Gorgonzola or other blue-veined cheese should be thinly sliced.

Hot fillings These could include crisply-fried bacon, frankfurters, pork sausages, herbed sausages, venison sausages and any other favourites; Lamb kebabs; or Stir-fried prawns (shrimp) in tomato sauce.

CIDER CUP

INGREDIENTS

2l/3½pt/8¾ cups dry cider, chilled

1l/1¾pt/4⅓ cups sparkling apple juice, chilled

300ml/½pt/1¼ cups sweet sherry

600ml/1pt/2½ cups soda water, chilled

225g/8oz/1 cup frozen blackberries, thawed

2 dessert apples, cored and thinly sliced

2tbsp lemon juice

1 Mix the cider, apple juice and sherry in a large punch bowl and, just before serving, pour on the soda water.

2 Add the blackberries and the apple slices tossed in lemon juice.

Serves 20–24

LEFT: Cider Cup, decorated with apple slices and blackberries.

OPPOSITE: Herb-flavoured Lamb Kebabs and warm pitta bread served with Barbecue Sauce.

LAMB KEBABS

These are particularly appropriate to serve in warm pitta bread, with shredded lettuce and onion rings.

INGREDIENTS

1kg/2¼lb lean lamb, trimmed and cut into 1.5-cm/½-in cubes
juice of 1 lemon

FOR THE MARINADE

3tbsp olive oil
1tsp dried oregano
½tsp dried thyme
2tbsp red wine vinegar
freshly ground black pepper

1 Mix the marinade ingredients together and pour the mixture into a large shallow dish.

2 Thread the lamb onto small wooden skewers and place them in the marinade. Spoon the liquid over the meat, cover and set aside for about 1 hour. Heat the grill (broiler) to medium.

3 Remove the skewers from the marinade and grill (broil) them for 6–7 minutes, turning them frequently and basting them with the marinade.

4 Transfer the kebabs to a warmed serving dish, sprinkle them with lemon juice and a few grindings of pepper.

STIR-FRIED PRAWNS (SHRIMP)

INGREDIENTS

5tbsp vegetable oil
4 cloves garlic, finely chopped
4 spring onions
1kg/2¼lb frozen prawns (shrimps), thawed
450g/1lb tomatoes, skinned and chopped
2tbsp soy sauce
1tsp sugar
1tsp cornflour (cornstarch)
1tbsp water

1 Heat the oil in a wok or frying pan until it is just beginning to smoke. Add the garlic and the onions and stir-fry over a high heat for 1 minute.

2 Add the prawns (shrimp) and stir-fry for 2–3 minutes, until they become firm. Remove the onions and prawns with a draining spoon and add the tomatoes, soy sauce and sugar.

3 Stir the cornflour (cornstarch) into the water, pour into the pan and cook over a moderate heat for 5–7 minutes, until the mixture forms a thick paste.

4 Return the onion and prawn (shrimp) mixture and just heat through. Serve hot.

Fills about 20 rolls

BARBECUE SAUCE

INGREDIENTS

3tbsp olive oil
1 large onion, finely chopped
1 red pepper, cored, seeded and chopped
2 cloves garlic, finely chopped
2tbsp tomato purée
225g/8oz can chopped tomatoes
2 bay leaves
1tsp dried oregano
salt and black pepper

1 Heat the oil in a pan and fry the onion, pepper and garlic over a moderate heat for about 3 minutes, until the onion is translucent.

2 Add the tomatoes, bay leaves and oregano and season with salt and pepper.

3 Bring to the boil and simmer for 10–15 minutes, until the mixture forms a paste.

4 Discard the bay leaves, and season.

Makes about 450ml/¾pt/2 cups

MULLED CLARET

A blend of claret, cider and orange juice, this mull can be varied to suit the occasion by increasing or decreasing the proportion of fruit juice or, to give the mull more pep, by adding up to 150ml/¼pt/⅔ cup brandy.

INGREDIENTS

1½l/2½pt/6¼ cups inexpensive
claret
600ml/1pt/2½ cups medium cider
300ml/½pt/1¼ cups orange juice
1 orange
5tbsp clear honey
2tbsp seedless raisins
2 clementines
a few cloves
4tbsp demerara (light brown)
sugar
grated nutmeg
2 cinnamon sticks

1 With a sharp knife or a rotary peeler, pare off a long strip of orange peel.

2 Place the peel, honey and raisins in a large pan. Stud the clementines with cloves and add them.

3 Grate a little nutmeg into the sugar and add to the pan with the cinnamon sticks. Pour on the wine and heat over a low heat, stirring until the sugar has dissolved and the honey melted.

RIGHT: *Mulled Claret makes a welcoming drink to break the ice.*

4 Pour in the cider and the orange juice and continue to heat the mull gently. Do not allow it to boil.

5 Warm a punch bowl or other serving bowl. Remove the clementines and cinnamon sticks and strain the mull into the bowl to remove the raisins. Add the clementines studded with cloves, and serve hot in warmed glasses or in glasses containing a silver spoon (to prevent the glass breaking). Grate a little nutmeg over each serving, if you wish.

Makes 16 150ml/¼pt glasses

JAMAICA SUNSET

This frothy blend of eggs, milk and spirits definitely comes into the just-before-bedtime category of drink.

INGREDIENTS
4 eggs, separated
2tbsp caster (superfine) sugar
4tbsp dark rum
4tbsp brandy
300ml/¹/₂pt/1¹/₄ cups milk, hot
(or according to the volume of the glasses)
nutmeg

2 Pour on the rum and brandy, 1tbsp of each in each glass.

1 Beat the egg yolks with the sugar. Beat the whites to soft peaks. Mix together and pour into 4 heatproof glasses.

3 Top up with hot milk. Grate nutmeg on top.

Serves 4

MULLED CIDER

Another way to impart the tangy flavour of orange or other citrus fruit zest – without using the whole fruit or a twist of peel – is to rub sugar lumps over the rind. The rough surface of the sugar acts as a grater and removes the essential oils from just below the surface.

INGREDIENTS
20 sugar lumps
2 oranges, well washed
1 lemon
1 apple, thickly sliced
a few cloves
1 cinnamon stick
1l/1³/₄pt/4¹/₃ cups medium cider
4tbsp brandy
a few fresh strawberries, sliced, to decorate

1 Rub the sugar lumps over the zest of the oranges and put the sugar into a pan. Squeeze the juice from the oranges and add to the pan. Squeeze the juice from the lemon and brush some over the apple slices to prevent them from discolouring. Add the remaining lemon juice to the pan. Stud the apple slices with cloves and add together with cinnamon, cider and brandy.

2 Heat over a low heat, stirring to dissolve the sugar.

3 Pour the mull into a warmed punch bowl or serving dish and float a few strawberries on to decorate. Serve in heated glasses.

Makes about 18 glasses

INDEX

ACKNOWLEDGEMENTS

THE AUTHOR and publishers would like to thank the following organizations and companies for their help and co-operation in the preparation of this book:

Appalacia, The Folk Art Shop, 14a George Street, St Albans, Herts, AL3 4ER, tel 0727 836796, for American folk art items including hand-carved wooden figures, tinware and quilted decorations

Bostik Ltd, Ulverscroft Road, Leicester, LE4 6BW, tel 0533 510015 for the hot glue gun and various adhesives used to create many of the designs

California Raisins for the raisins used in the puddings, mincemeat, etc.

Danish Bacon Council for gammon bacon joints

Evans Kitchen Shop, 19 High Street, Halstead, Essex CO9 2AS, tel 0787 473967, for the loan of china, glass and other accessories

C.M. Offrey & Son Ltd, Fir Tree Place, Church Road, Ashford, Middx, TW15 2PH, tel 0784 247281, for the wide selection of ribbons

Paperchase, 213 Tottenham Court Road, London W1P 9AF, tel 071 581 8496, for the tree baubles and many of the decorative items

Prices Patent Candle Co Ltd, 1258 London Road, London SW16 4EE, tel 081 764 0640, for so many of the candles in the photographs

The author would also like to thank the following people for their help in so many ways:
Suzanne Ardley, Nelson Hargreaves, Margaret Jack, David Suckling, Anthony Thomas, Douglas Westland.

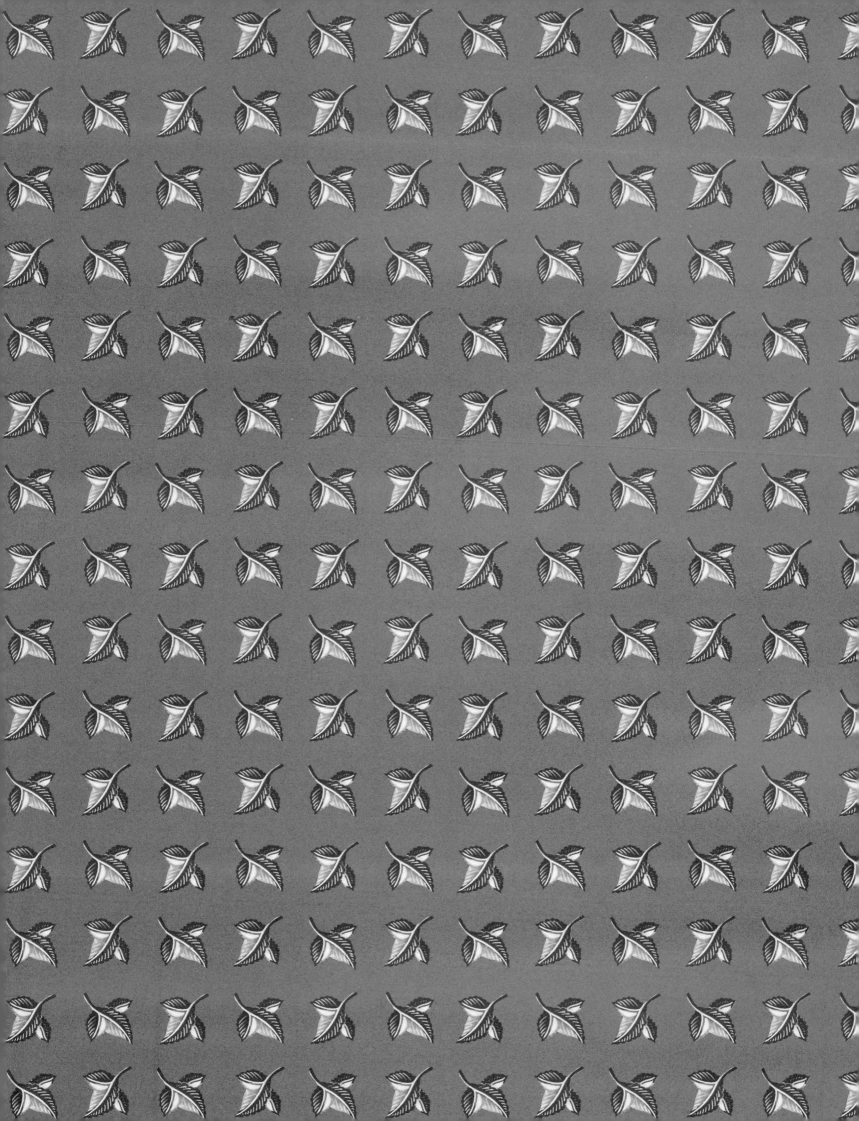